Thanks for Your trust!

One of the best ways to educate children is entertain them at the same time.

Activities such as coloring will improve your child's pencil grip, as well as helping them to relax, self regulate their mood and develop their imagination.

Moreover they will improve hand-eye coordination.

We wish You great time with our activity book!

We will be glad if You will get us a comment

THIS BOOK
belongs to

○○○○○○○○○○○○○○○○○○○

A A A A A A A

A A A A

APPLE APPLE

A A A A A A A A A

A A A A A A

APPLE APPLE APPLE

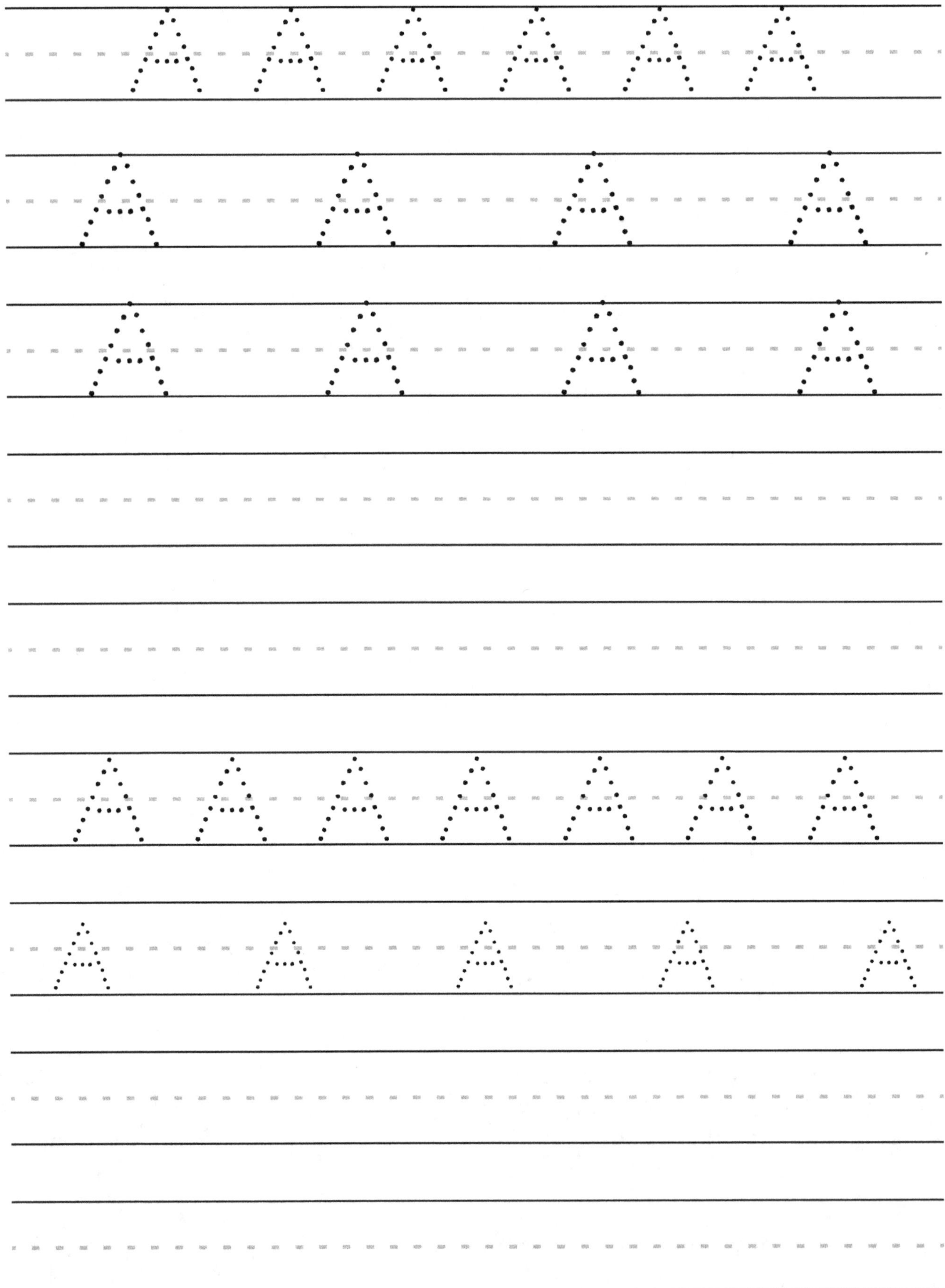

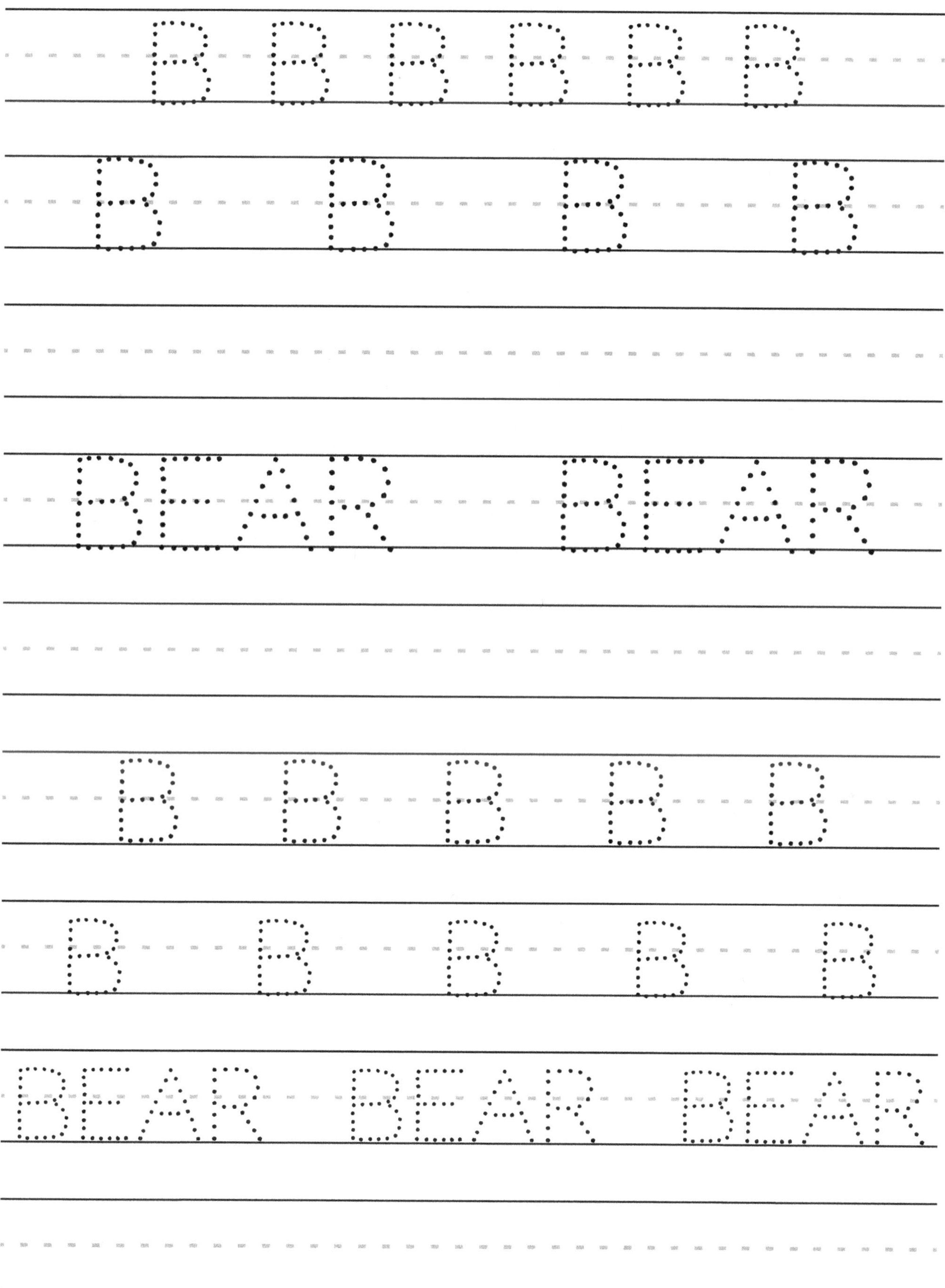

B B B B B B

B B B B

B B B B

B B B B B B B

B B B B B B

C C C C C C

C C C C

CAR CAR

C C C C C C C

C C C C C C

CAR CAR CAR

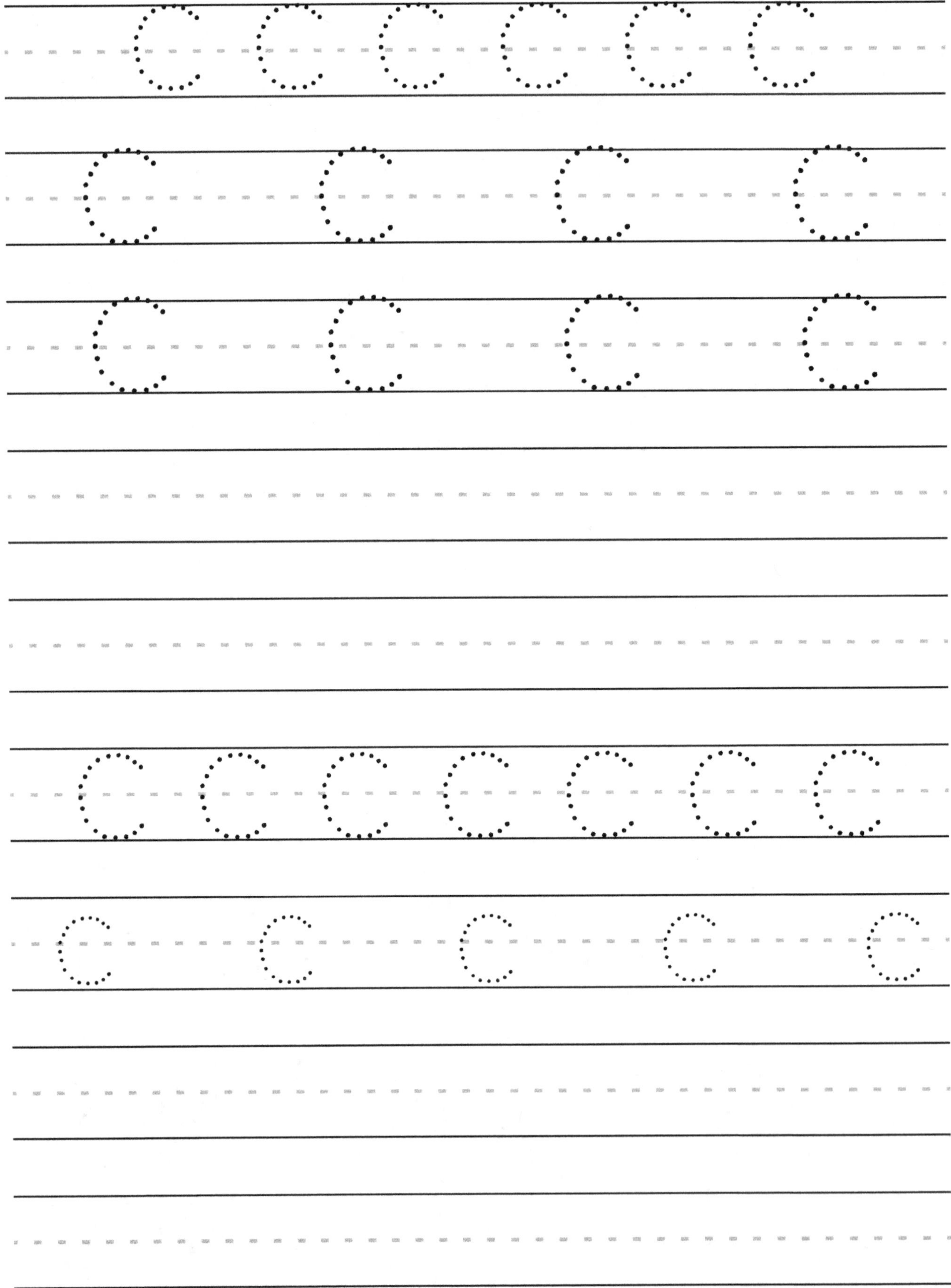

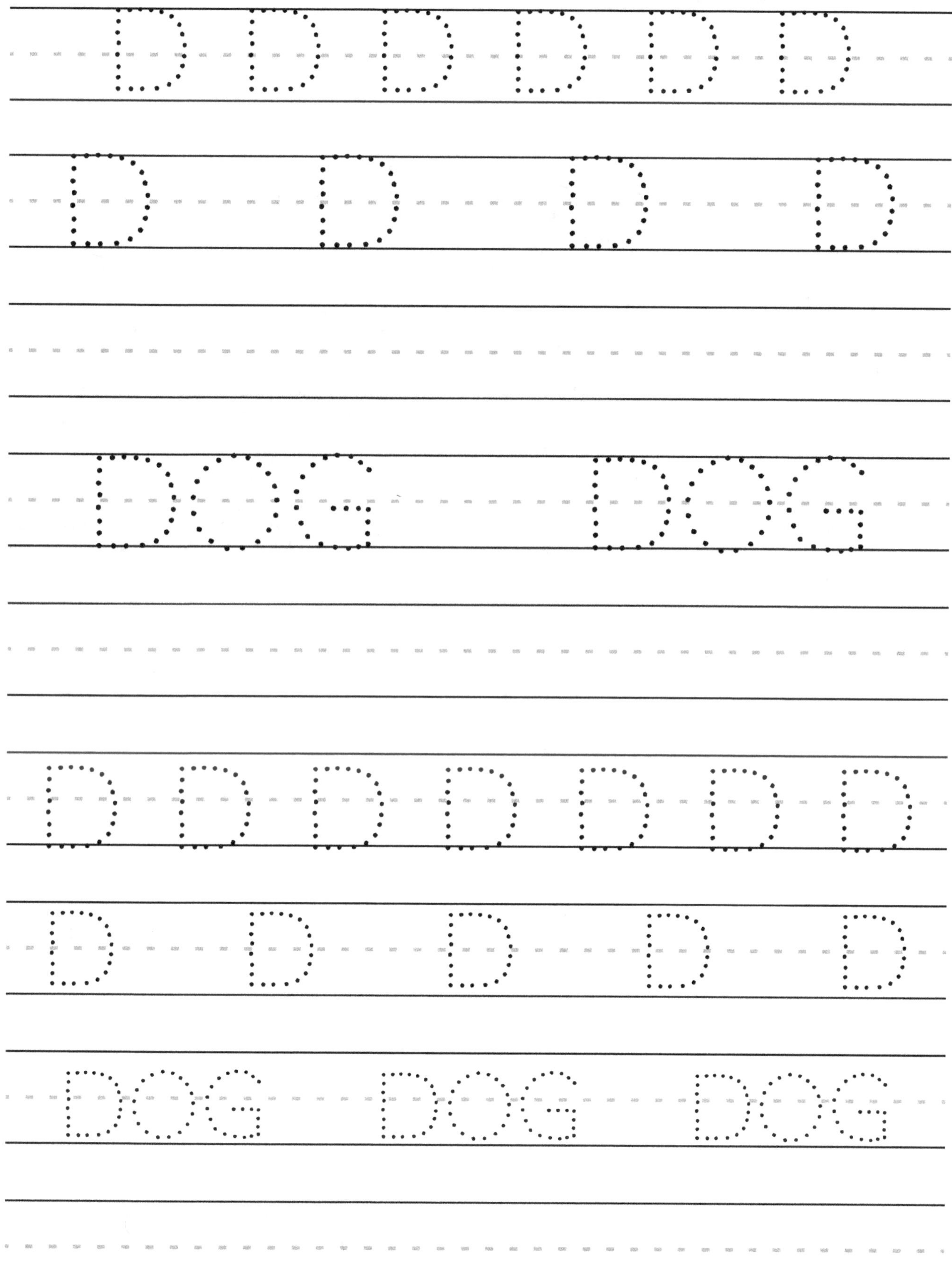

D D D D D D

D D D D

D D D D

D D D D D D D

D D D D D

E E E E E E E

E E E E

ELEPHANT

E E E E E E E

E E E E E E

ELEPHANT

E E E E E E

E E E E

E E E E

E E E E E E E

E E E E E

F F F F F F

F F F F

FROG FROG

F F F F F F

F F F F F

FROG FROG FROG

F F F F F F

F F F F

F F F F

F F F F F F F

F F F F F

G G G G G G

G G G G

GOAT GOAT

G G G G G G

G G G G G G

GOAT GOAT GOAT

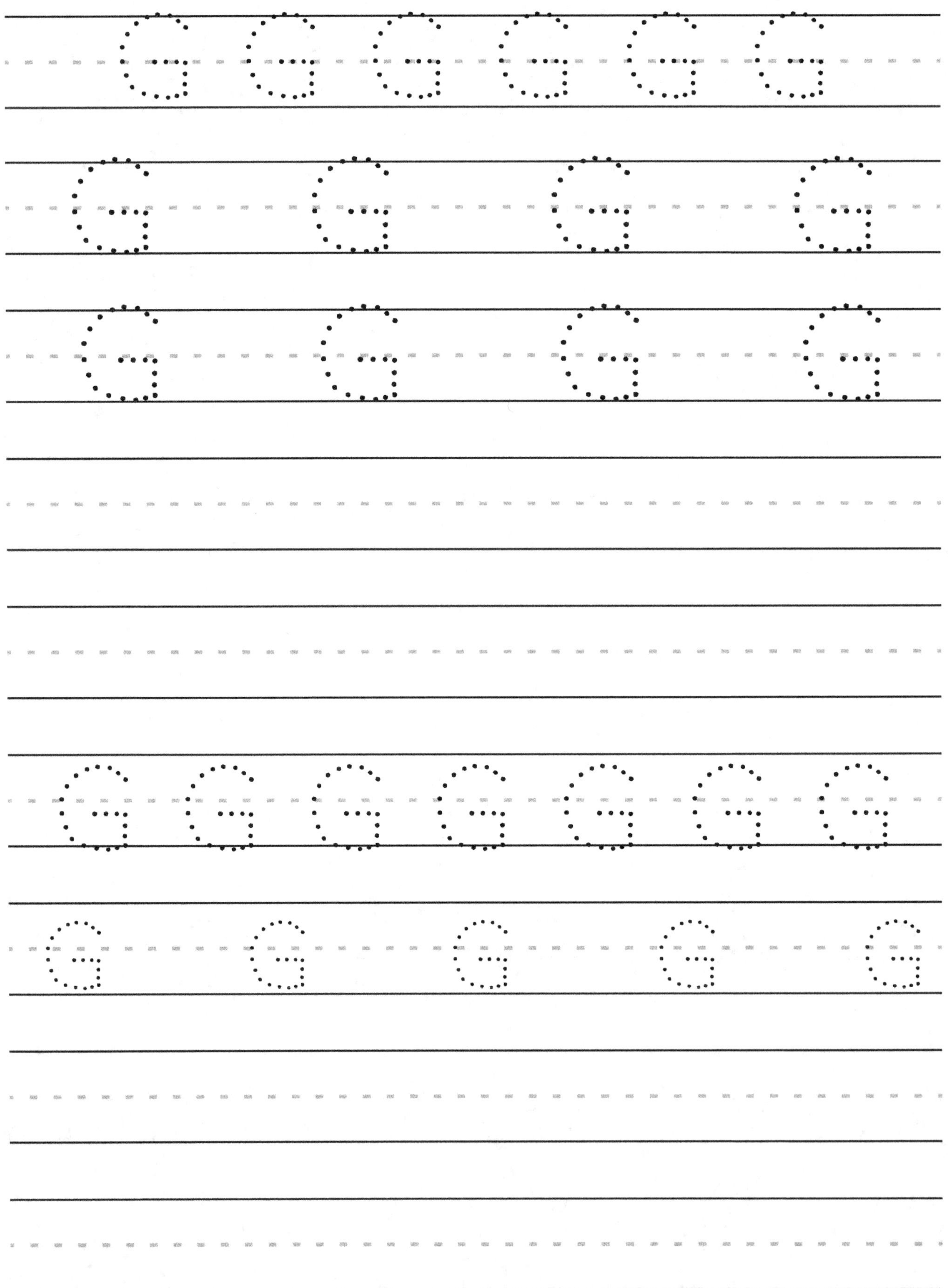

H H H H H H H

H H H H

HIPPO HIPPO

H H H H H H H H

H H H H H H

HIPPO HIPPO

H H H H H H H

H H H H

H H H H

H H H H H H H

H H H H H

I I I I I

I I I I I

IGLOO

I I I I

I I I I I I

IGLOO   IGLOO

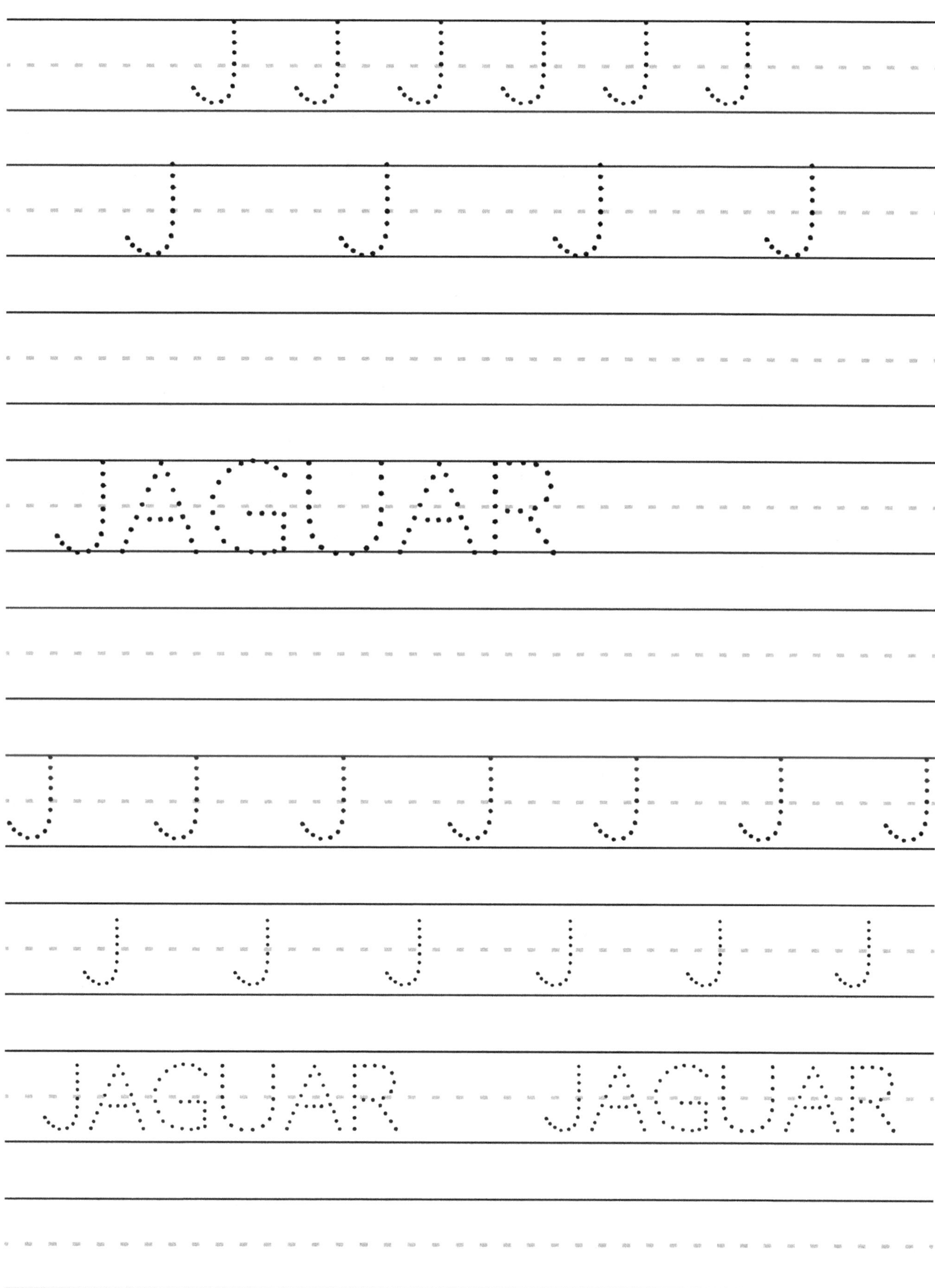

J J J J J J
J J J J
JAGUAR
J J J J J J J
J J J J J J
JAGUAR   JAGUAR

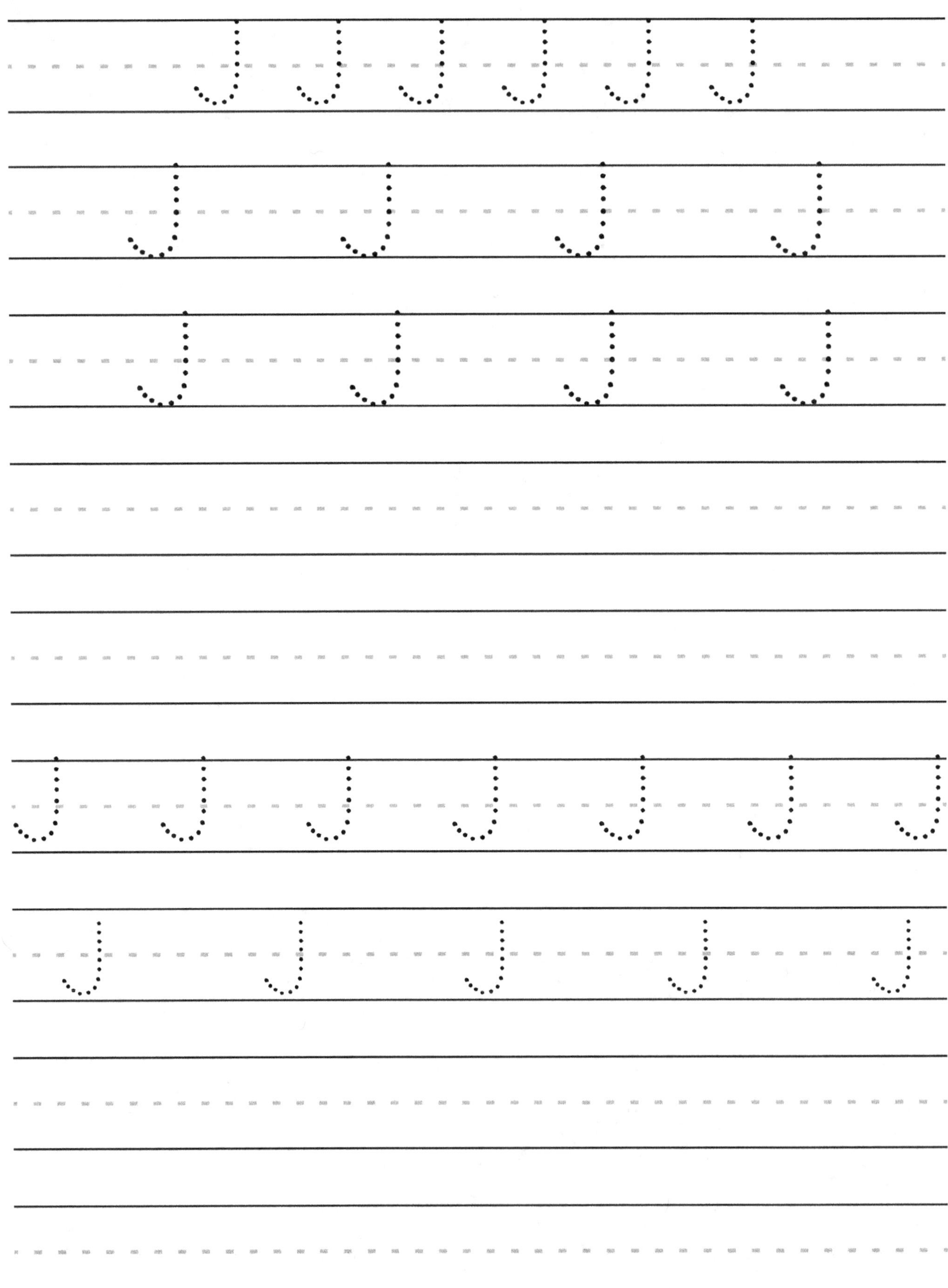

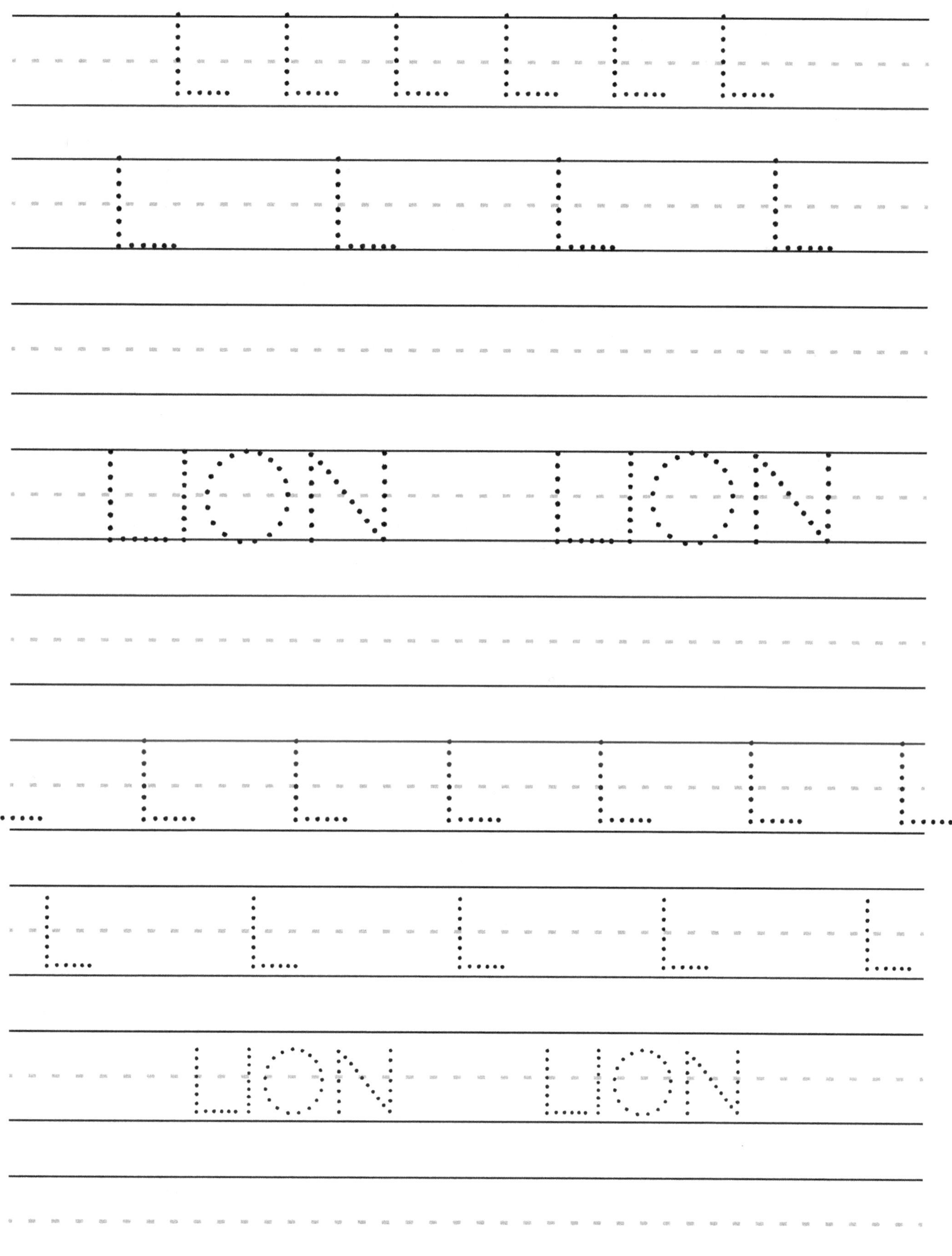

L L L L L L

L L L L

L L L L

L L L L L L L L

L L L L L

M M M M M M
M M M M M
MONKEY
M M M M M M M
M M M M M
MONKEY MONKEY

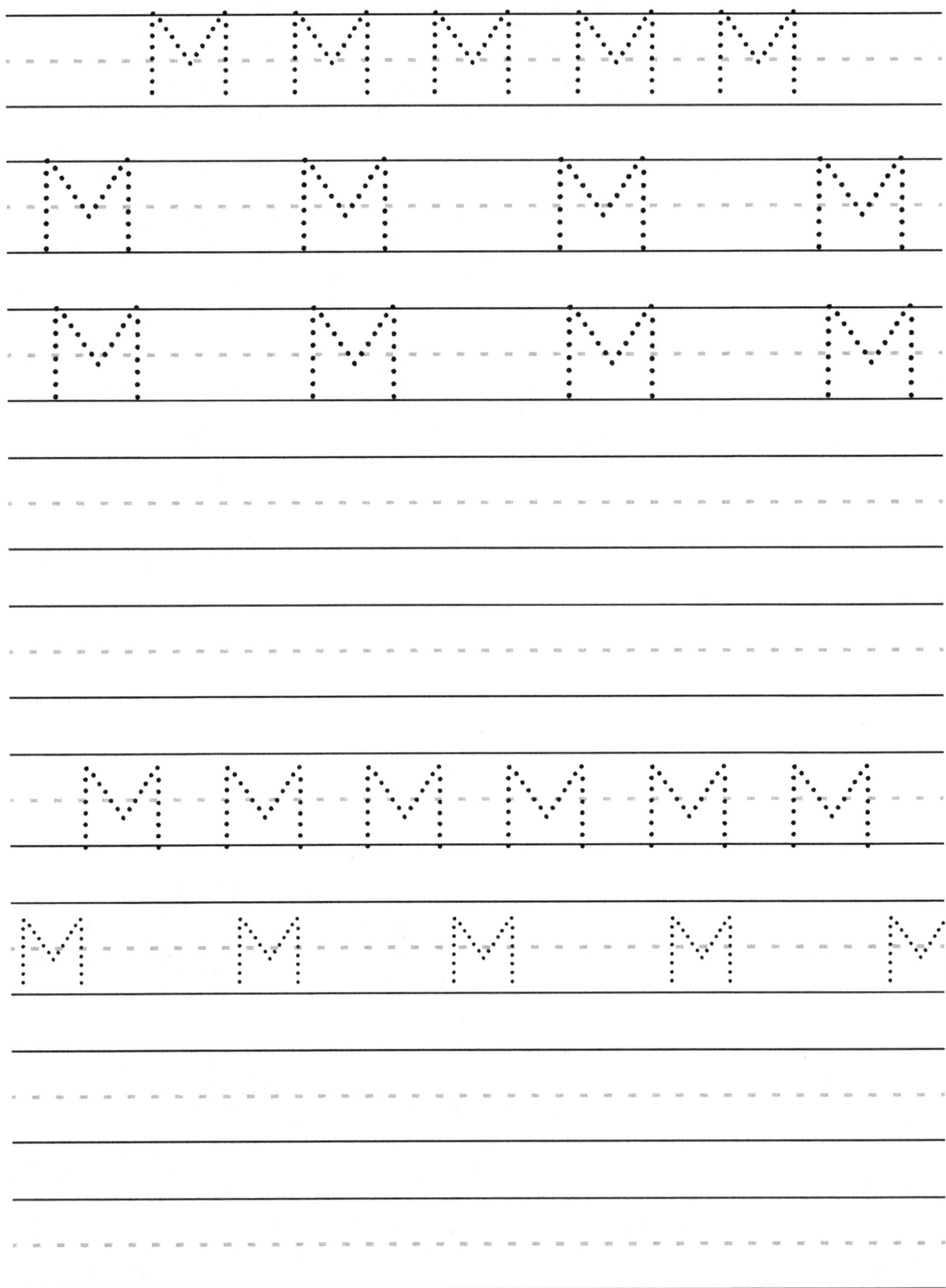

N N N N N N N N

N N N N

N N N N

N N N N N N N N

N N N N N

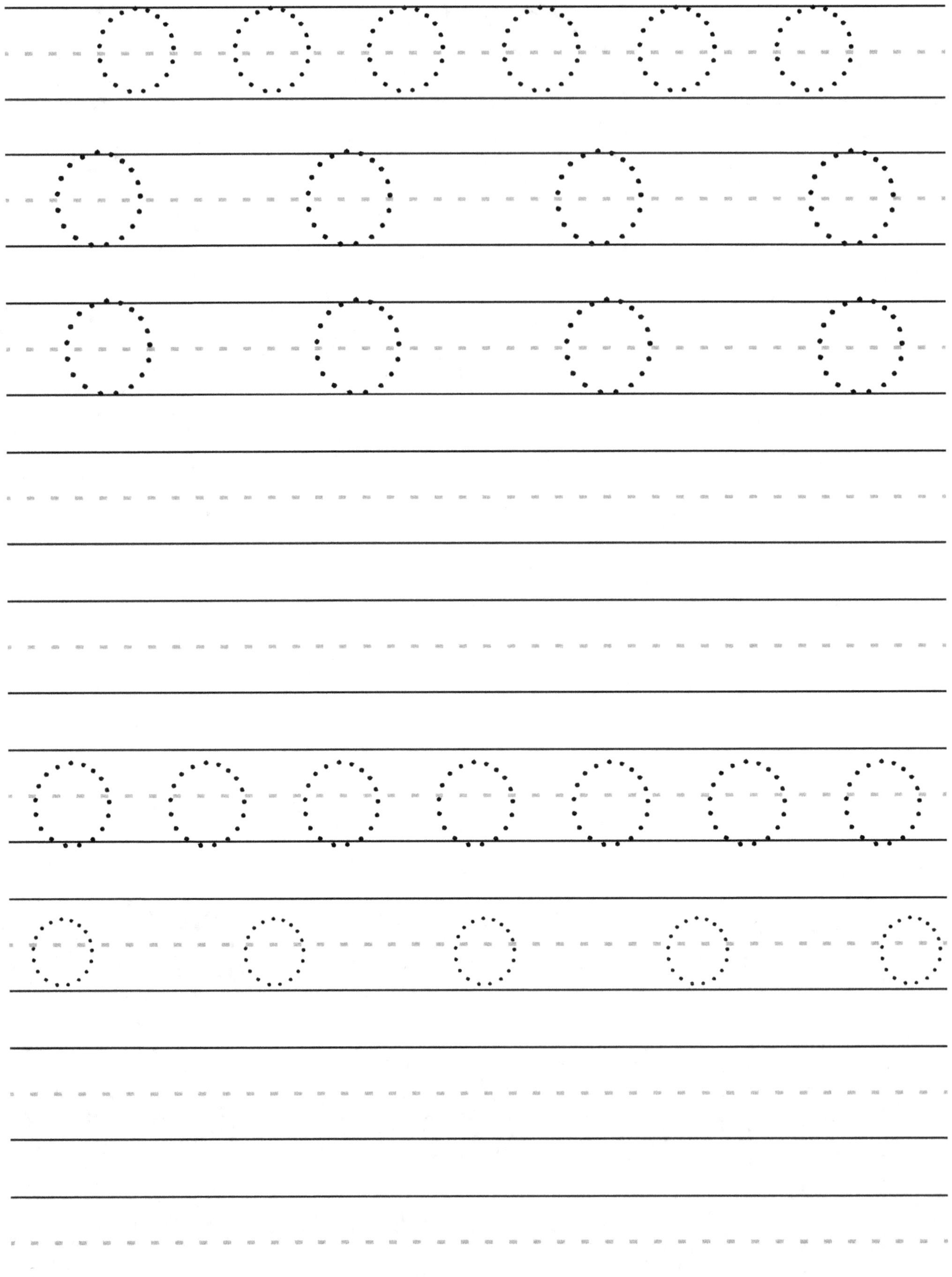

P P P P P P

P P P P

PEAR PEAR

P P P P P P P

P P P P P P

PEAR PEAR PEAR

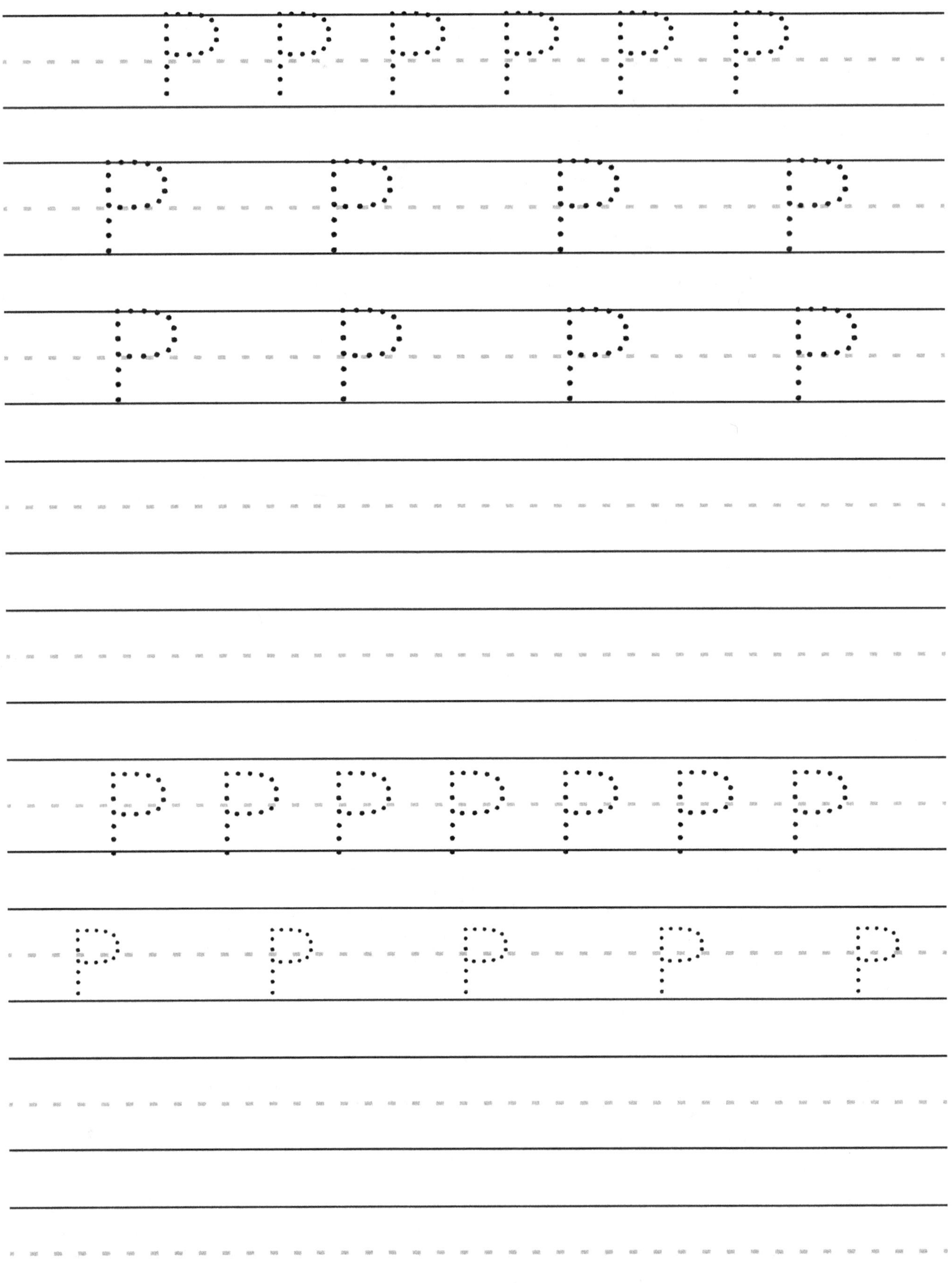

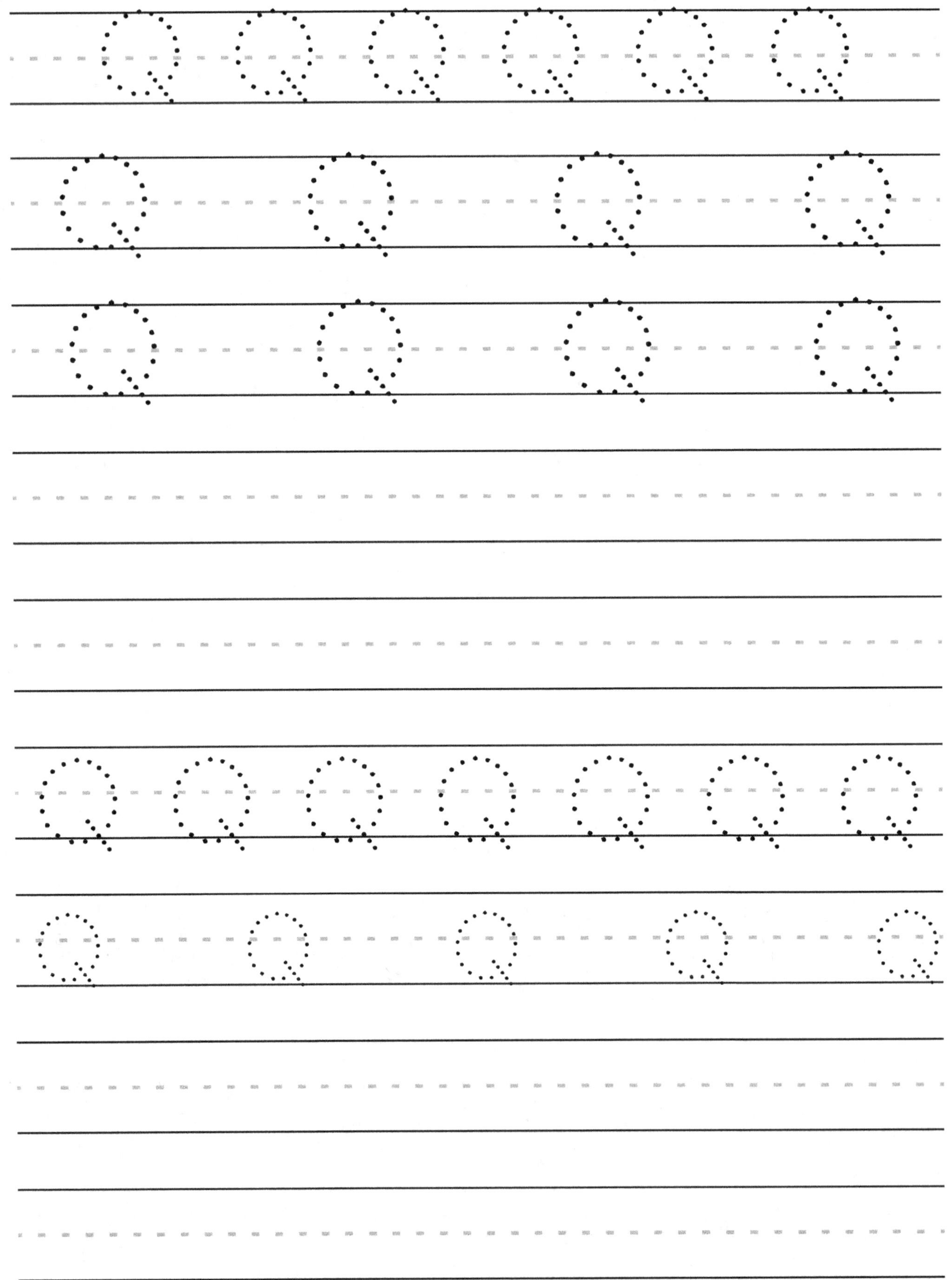

R R R R R R R

R   R   R   R

RABBIT RABBIT

R R R R R R R

R   R   R   R   R

RABBIT   RABBIT

R R R R R R R R

R R R R

R R R R

R R R R R R R R

R R R R R

S S S S S S

S S S S S

SHARK SHARK

S S S S S S S

S S S S S S

SHARK SHARK

S S S S S S

S S S S

S S S S

S S S S S S

S S S S S S

T T T T T T T

T T T T

TRUCK TRUCK

T T T T T T T

T T T T T

TRUCK TRUCK

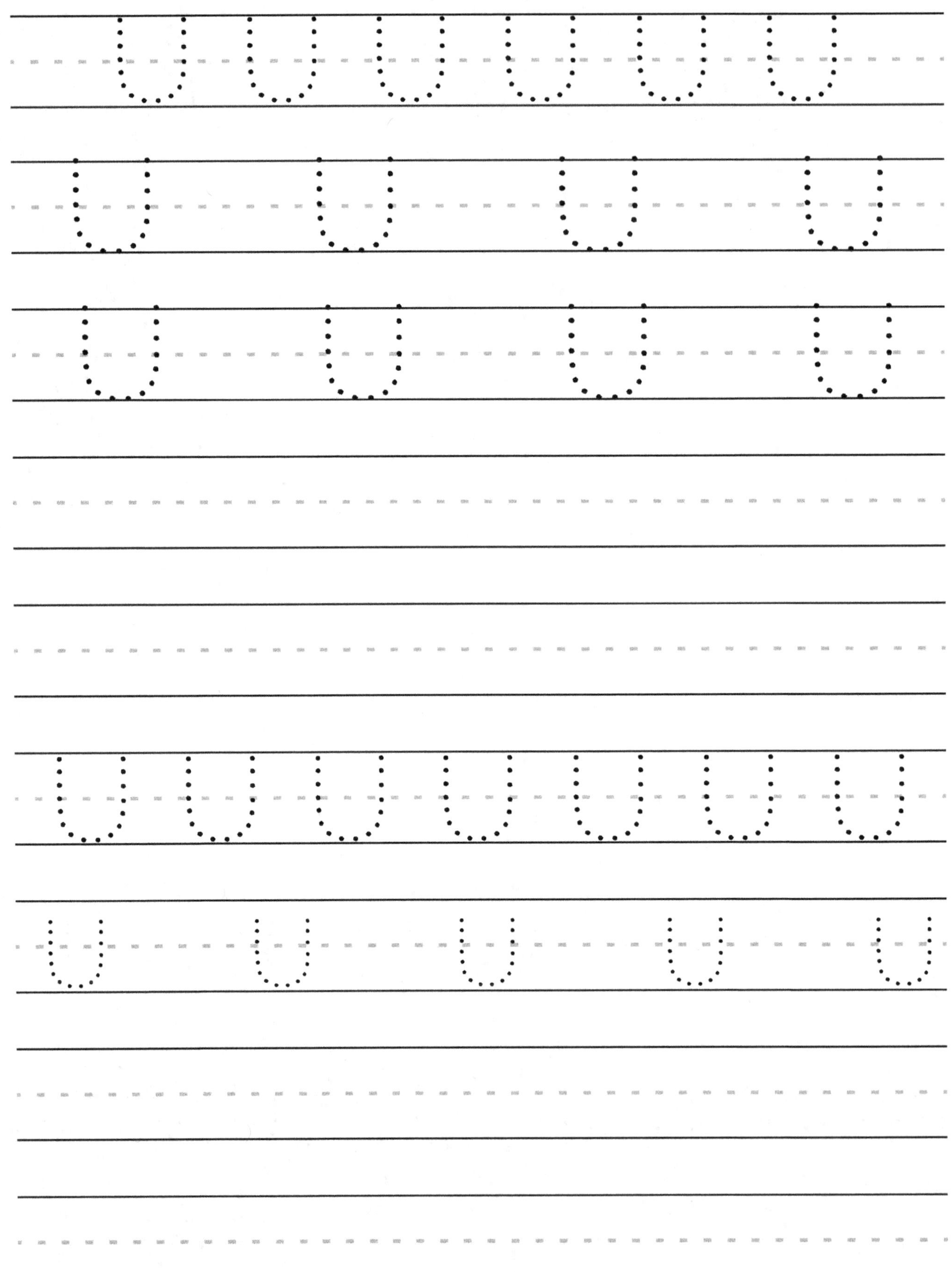

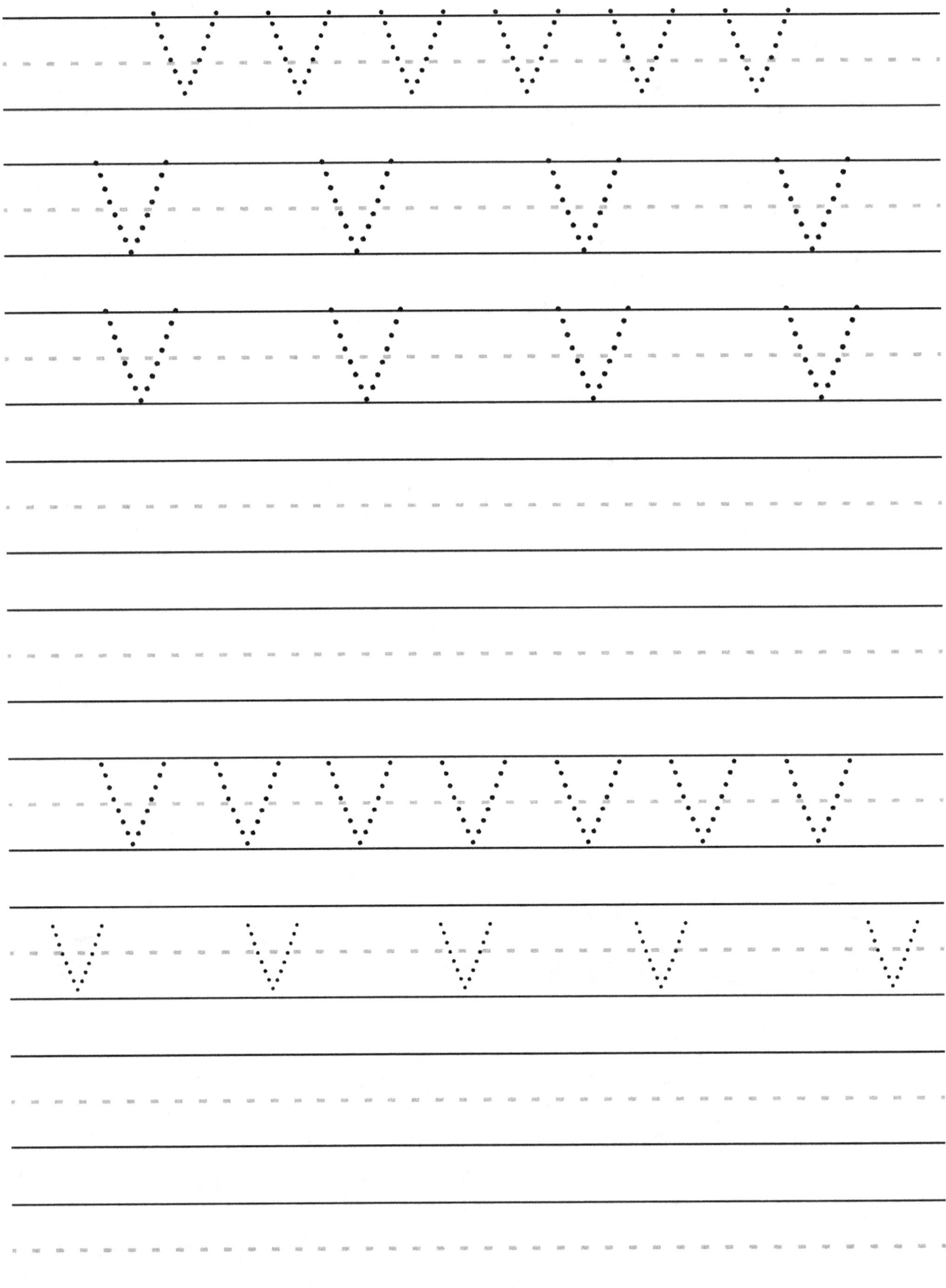

W W W W

W W W W

WHALE

W W W W W W W

W W W W W W

WHALE WHALE

W W W W

W W W W

W W W W

W W W W W W W

W W W W W

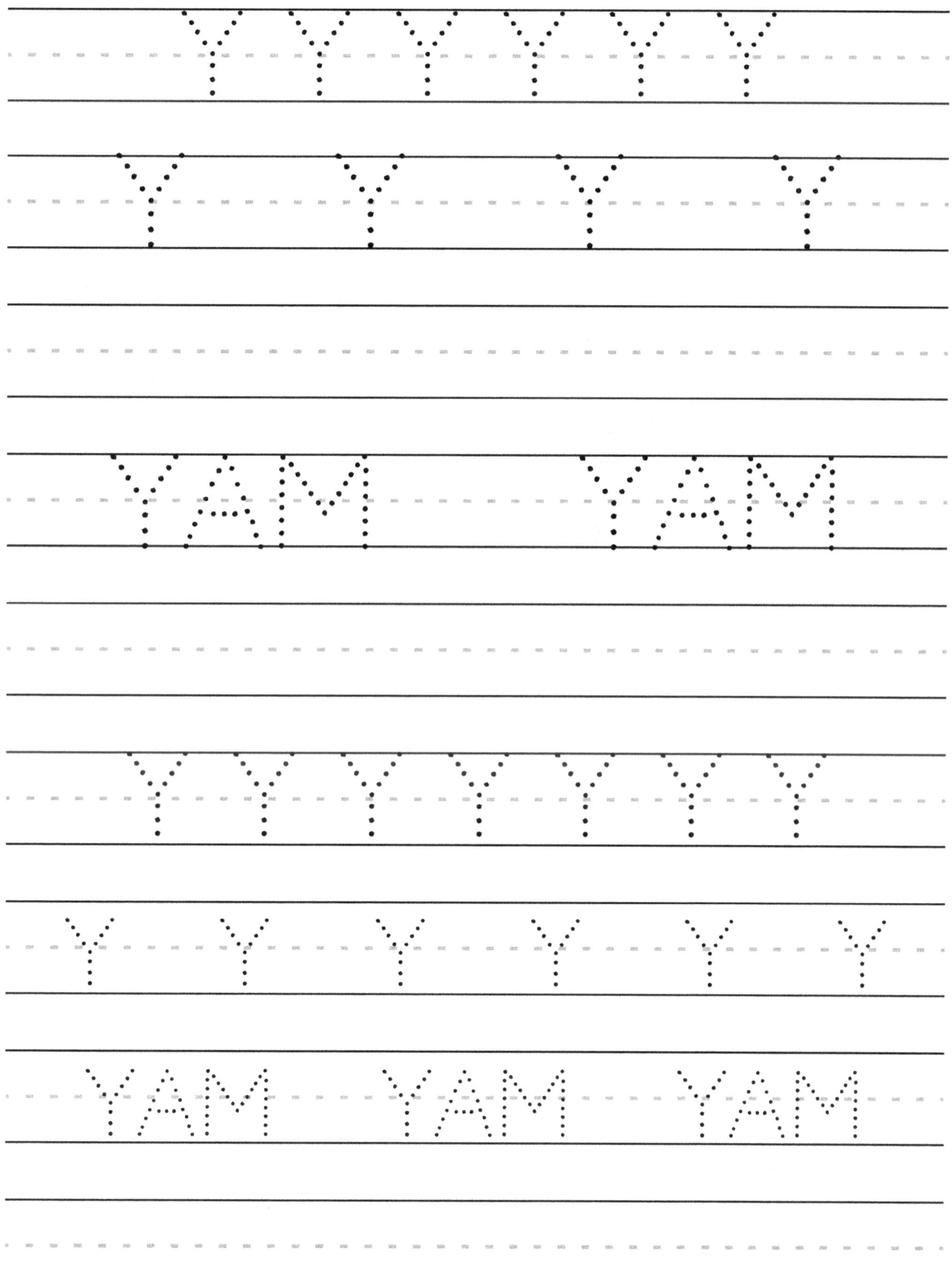

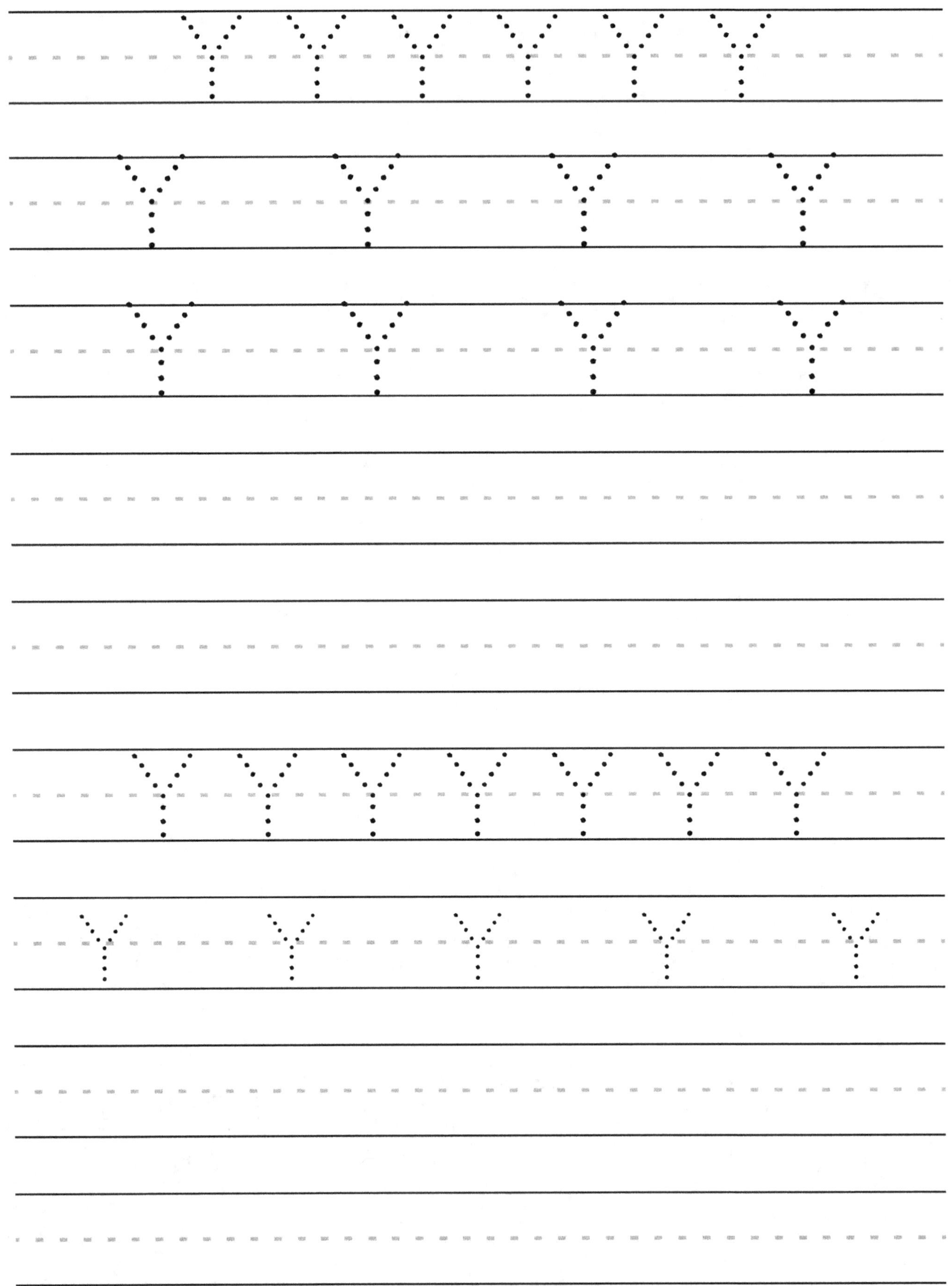

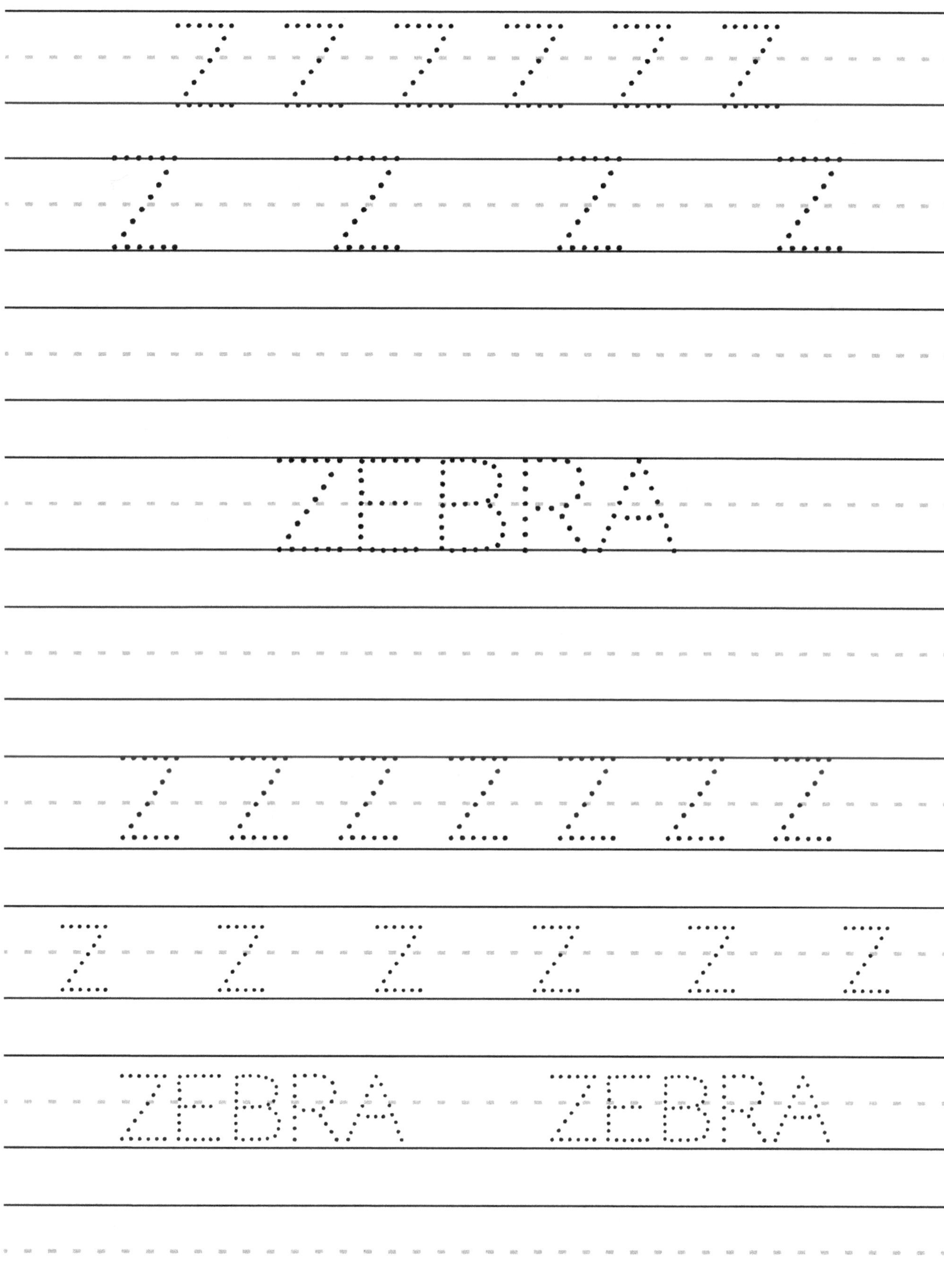

5 5 5 5 5 5 5

6 6 6 6 6 6 6

A

B

C

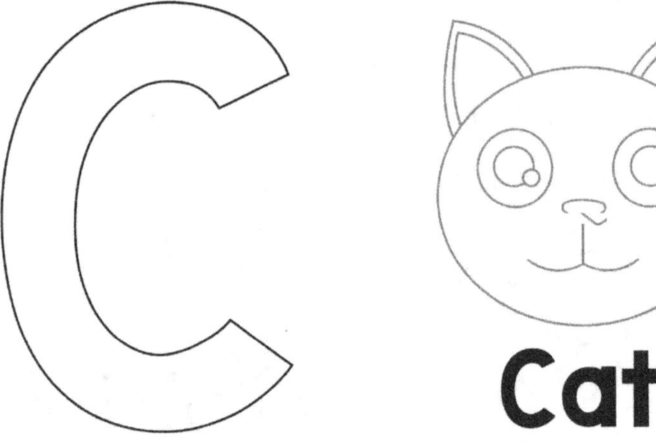

Cat

C

D

Cat

D

E

Egg

E

F

Flower

G

Game

G

H

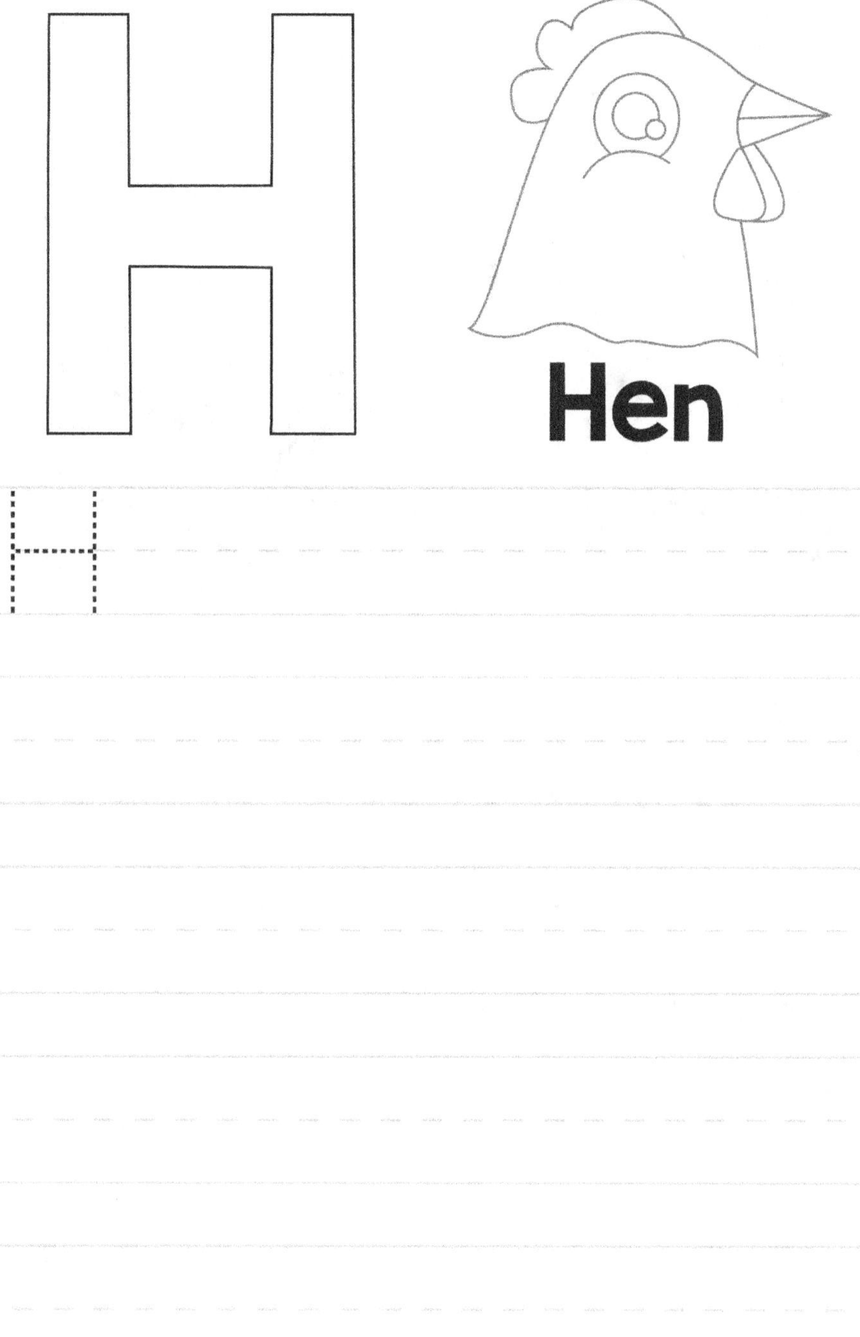

Hen

I

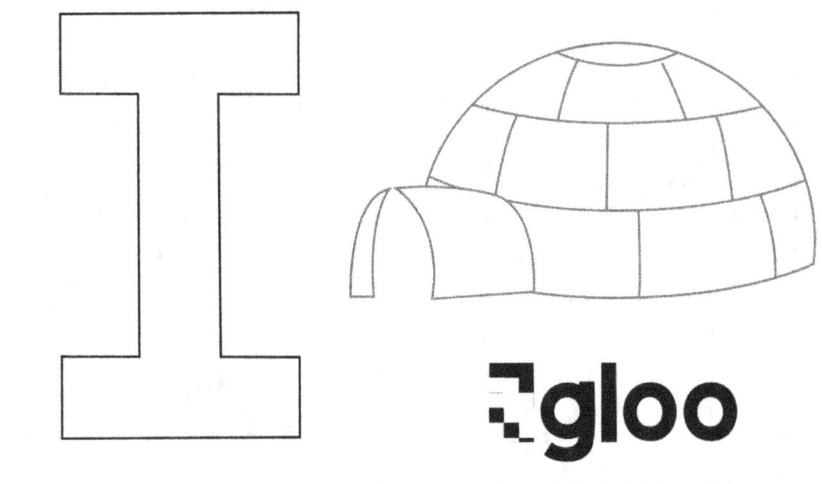

Jar

K

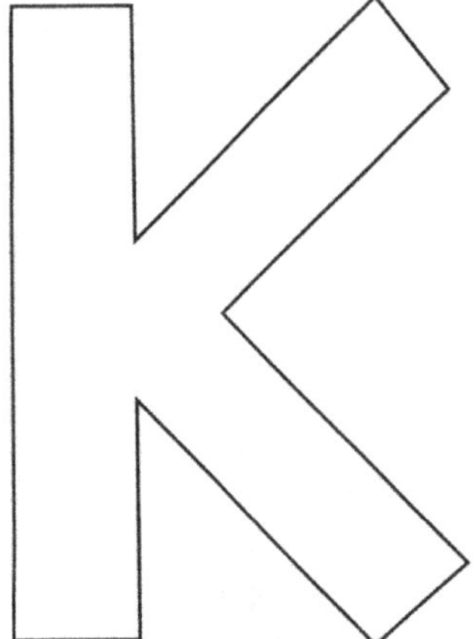

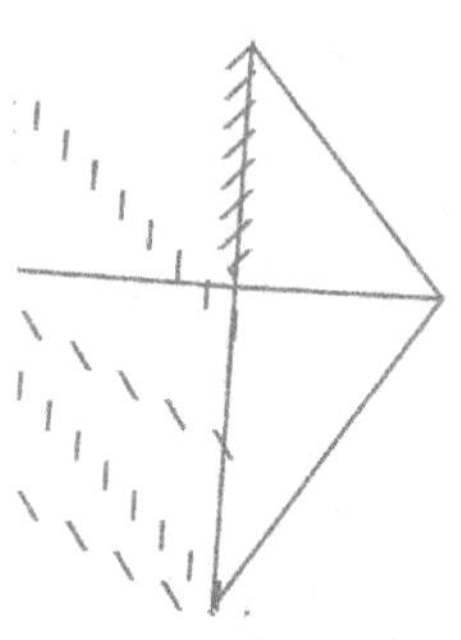

Kite

K

L

Lady bug

Mango

N

Night

O

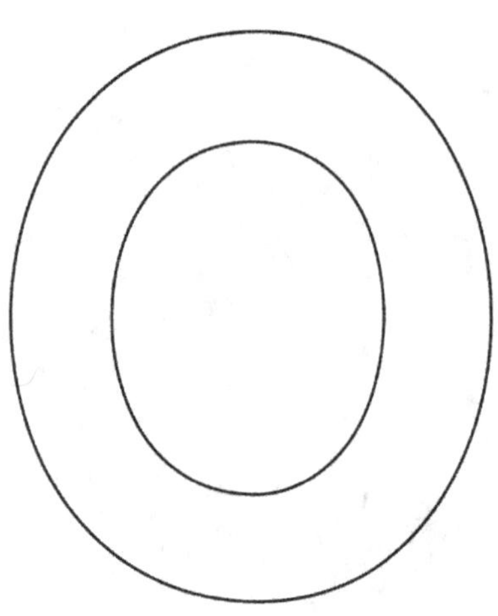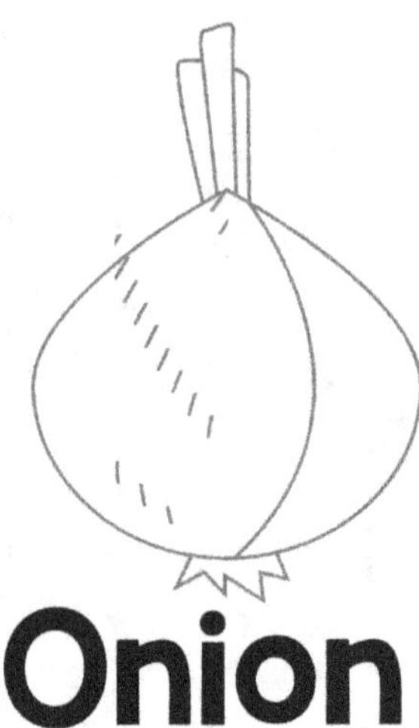

Onion

P

Pumpkin

P

Q

Quilting

R

R

S

T

Table

U

Umbrella

V

Valentines

W

Water

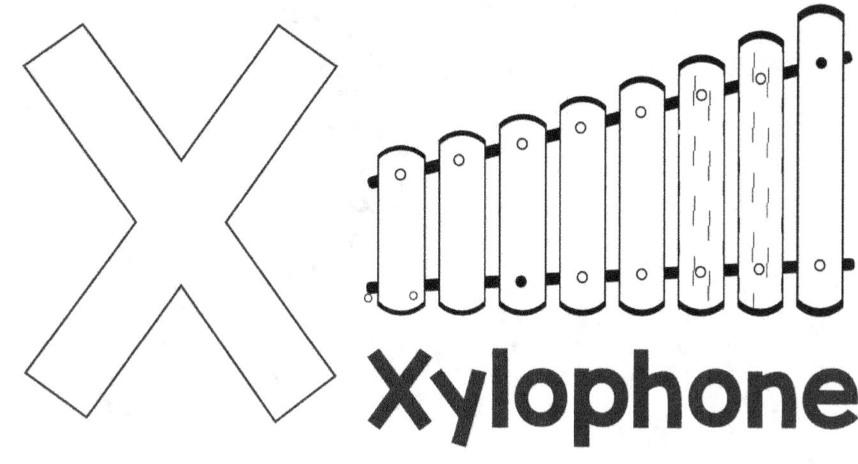

Xylophone

Y

Z

Zig Zag

Let's Start warming Up:

O

Trace the Number 0

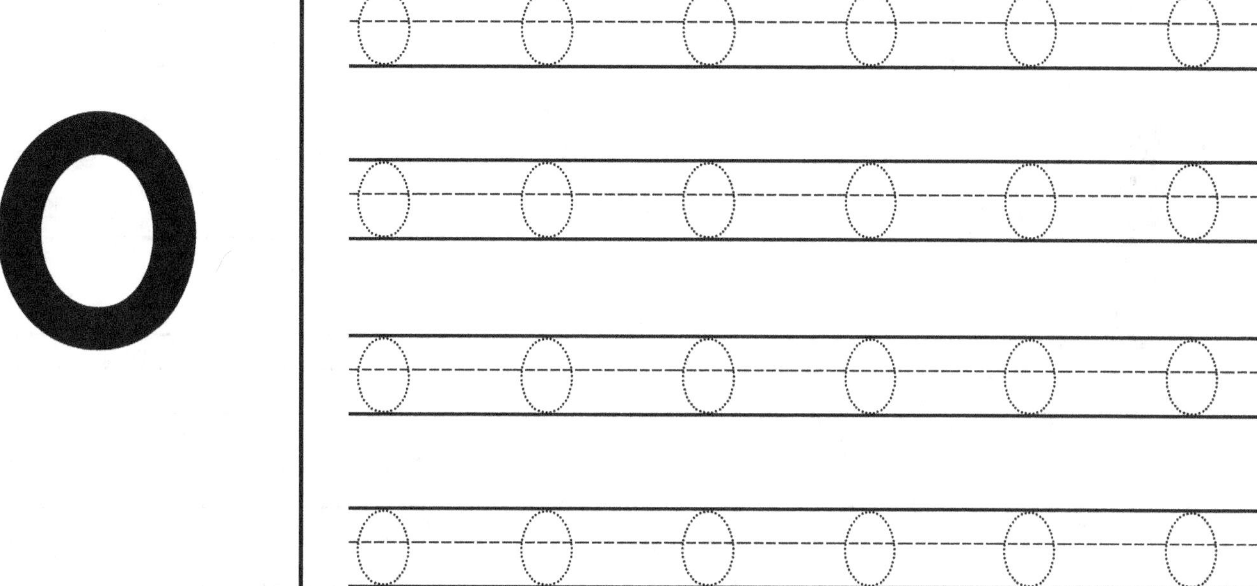

Trace the word Zero

Zero

Trace the Number 1

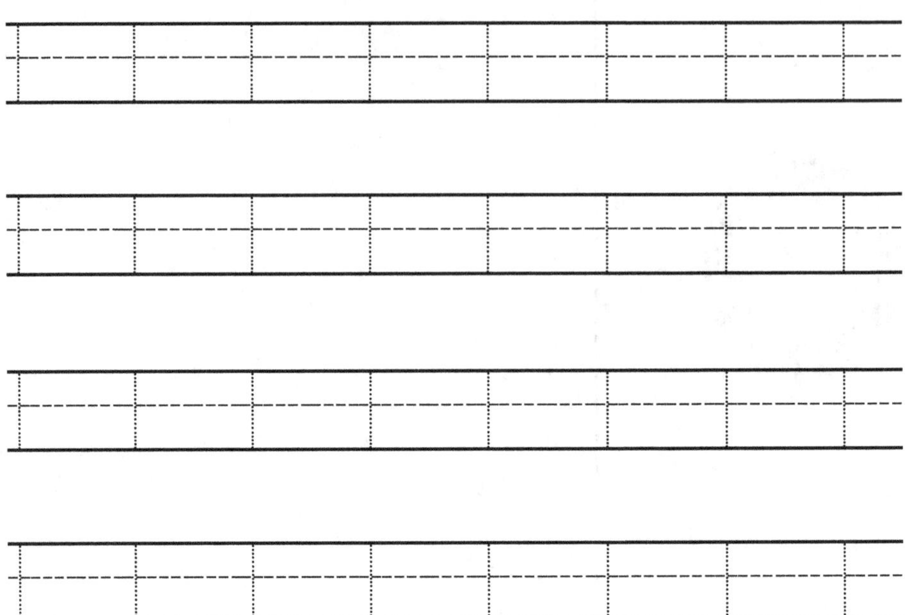

Trace the word One

1

Write Number 1

1 1
1 1
1 1
1 1

One

Color One Orange

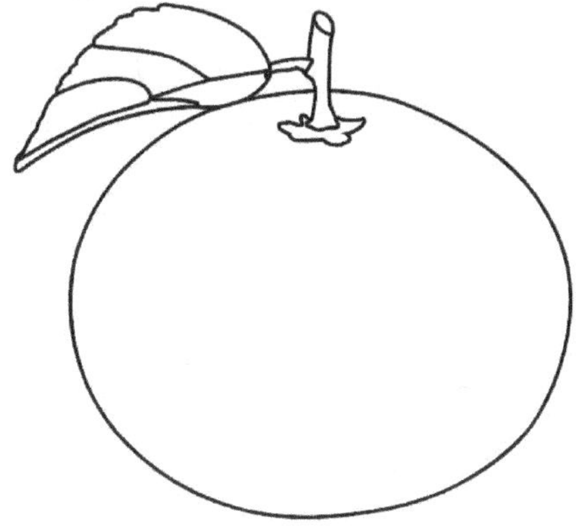

2

Trace the Number 2

Two

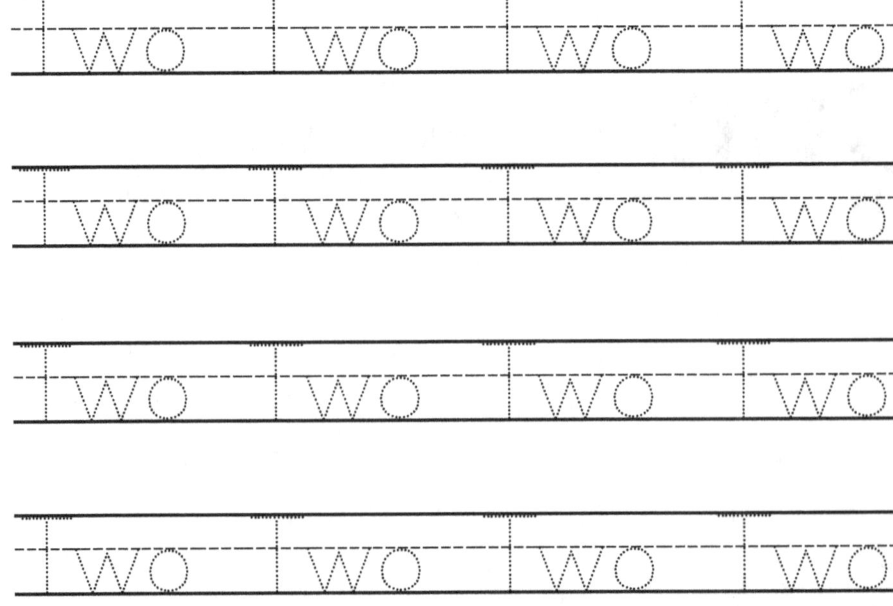

Trace the word Two

2

Two

Color Two Apples

3

Trace the Number 3

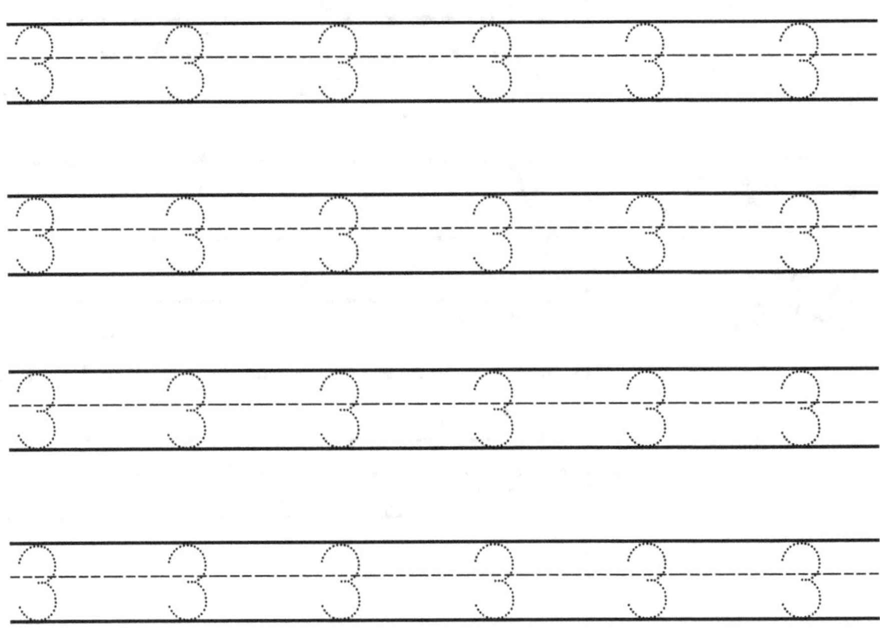

Three

Trace the word Three

3

Write Number 3

3
3
3
3

Three

Color Three Pears

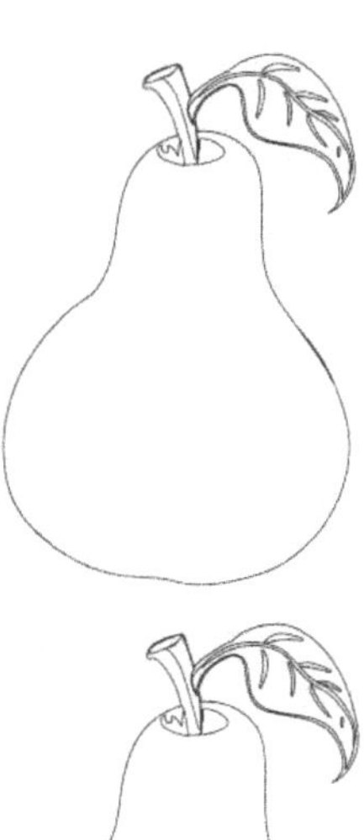

Trace the Number 4

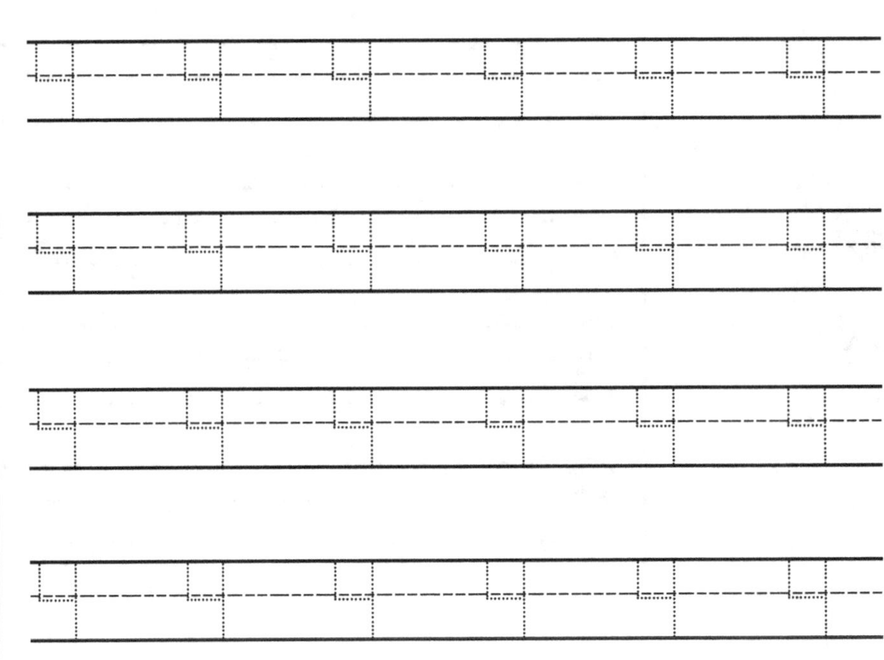

Trace the word Four

4

Write Number 4

4
4
4
4

Four

Color Four water Melon slices

Trace the Number 5

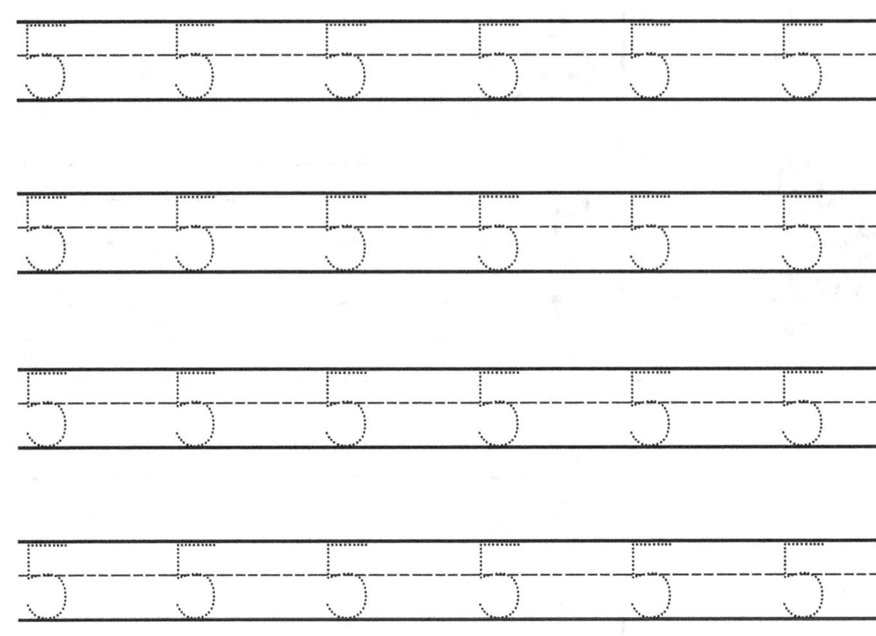

Trace the word Five

5

Five

Trace the Number 6

Trace the word Six

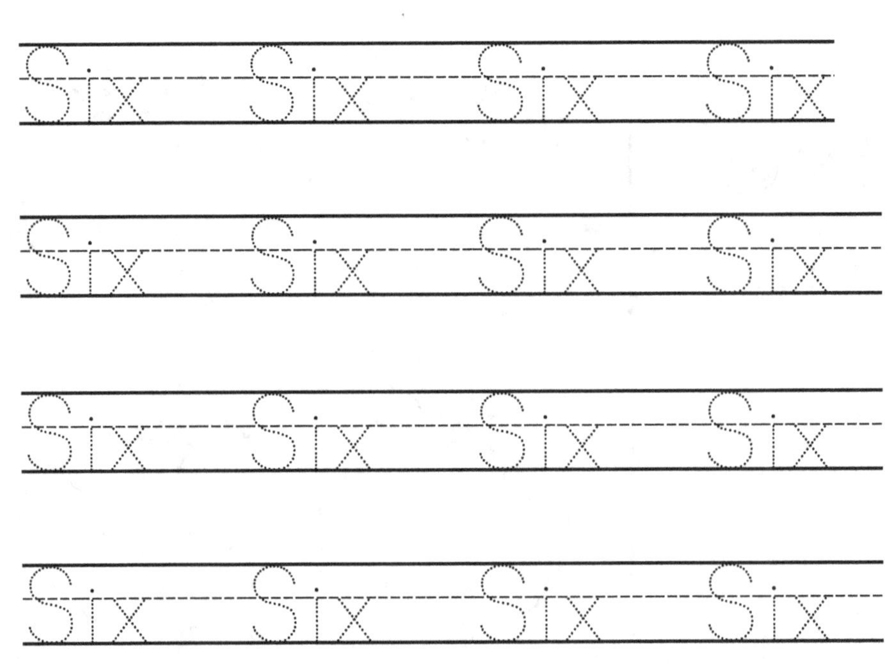

6

Write Number 6

6
6
6
6

Six

Color Six Carrots

7

Trace the Number 7

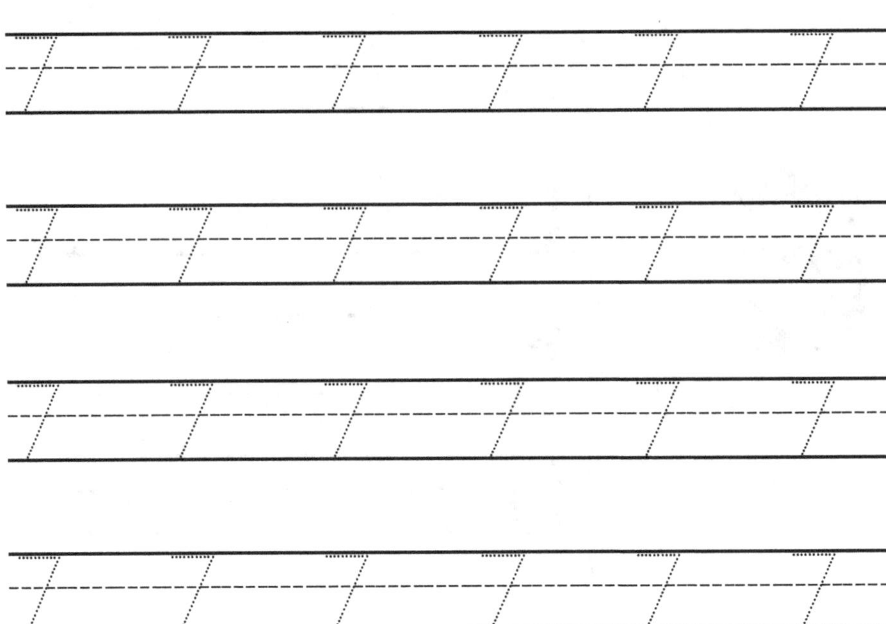

Trace the word Seven

Seven

7

Write Number 7

7
7
7
7

Seven

Color Seven Pumpkins

Trace the Number 8

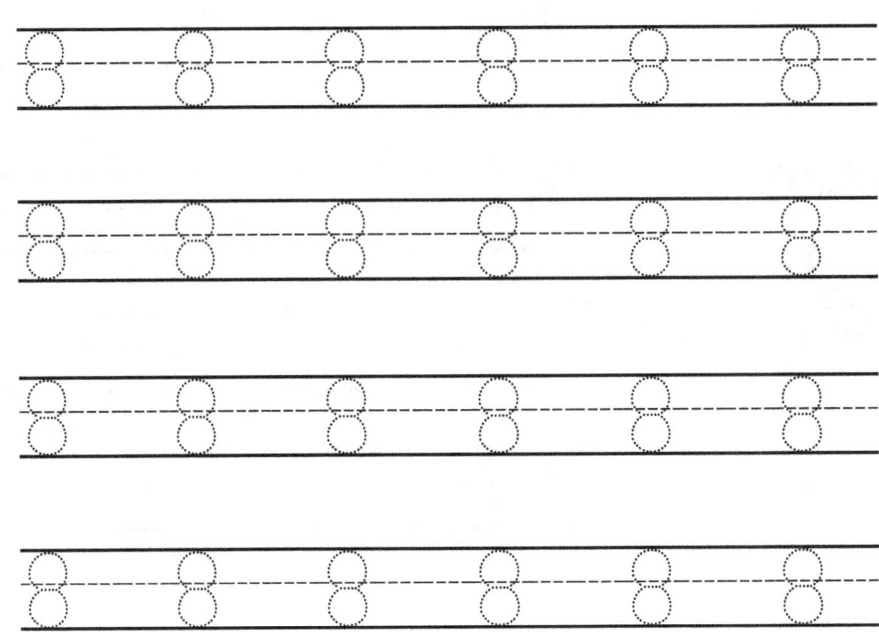

Trace the word Eight

8

Write Number 8

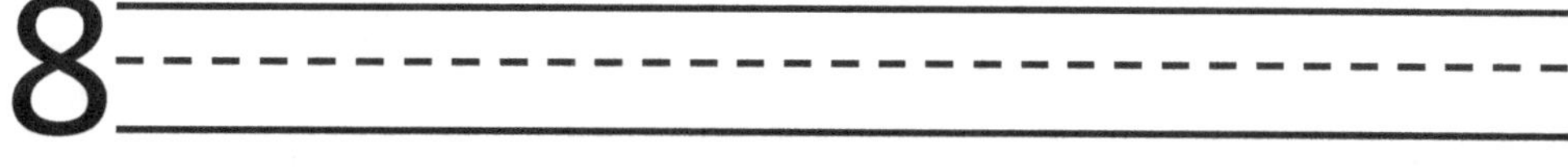

8 ————————————————
8 ————————————————
8 ————————————————
8 ————————————————

Eight

Color Eight Strawberries

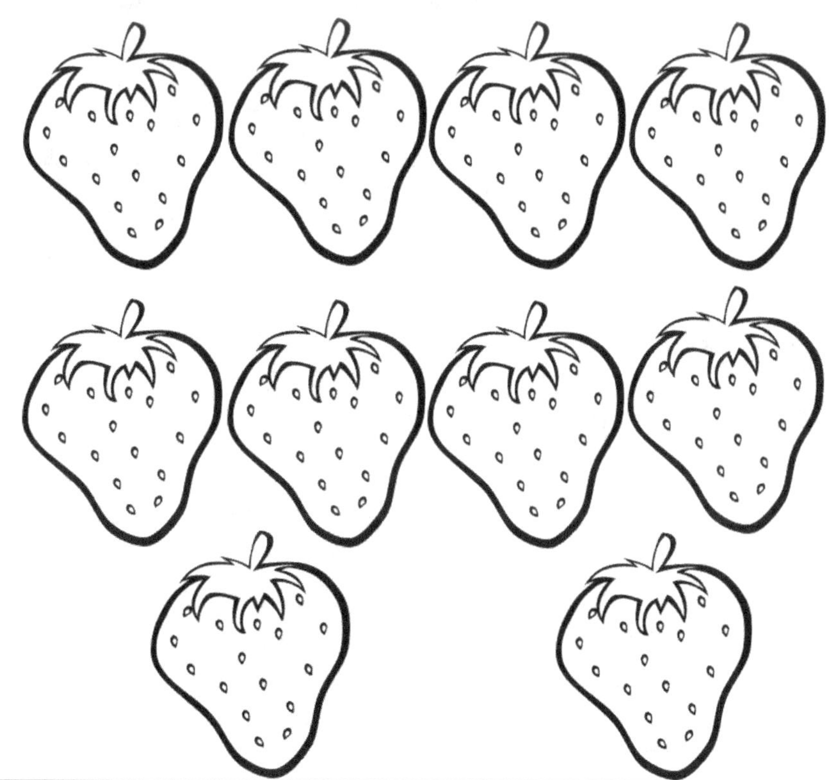

Trace the Number 9

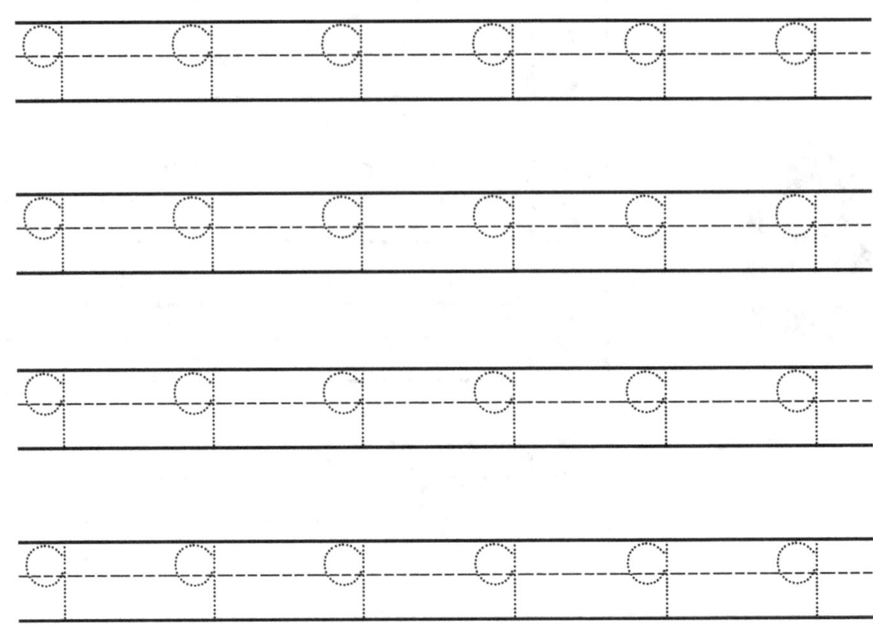

Trace the word Nine

9

Write Number 9

9
9
9
9

Nine

Color nine Spikes of wheat

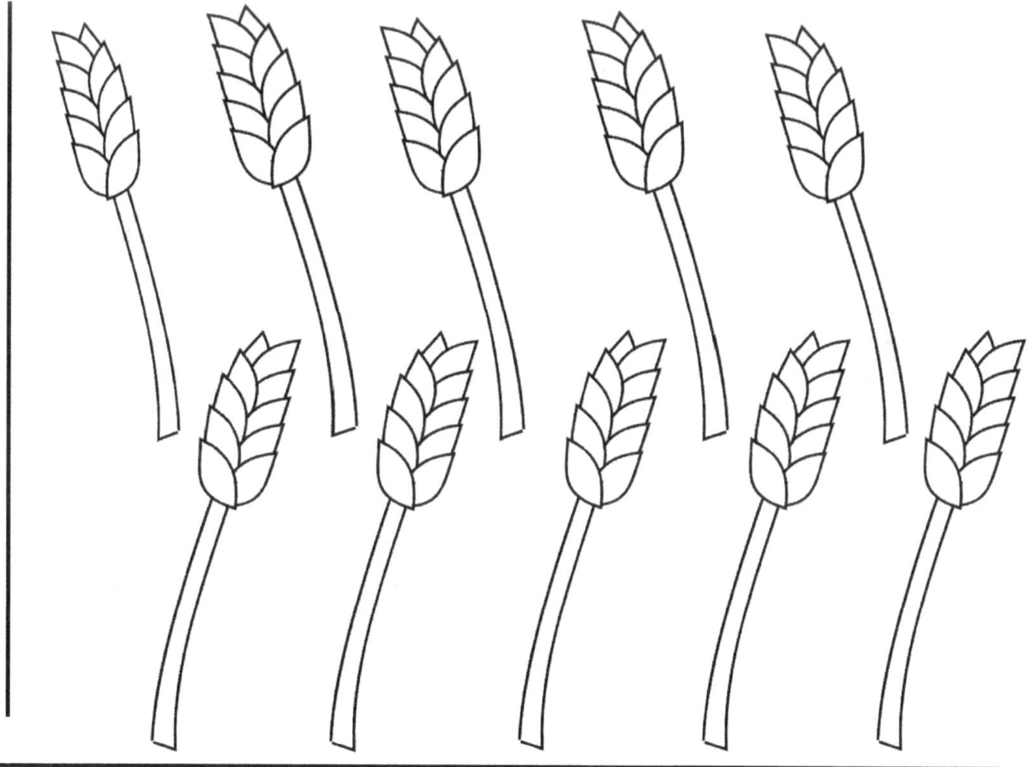

Trace the Number 10

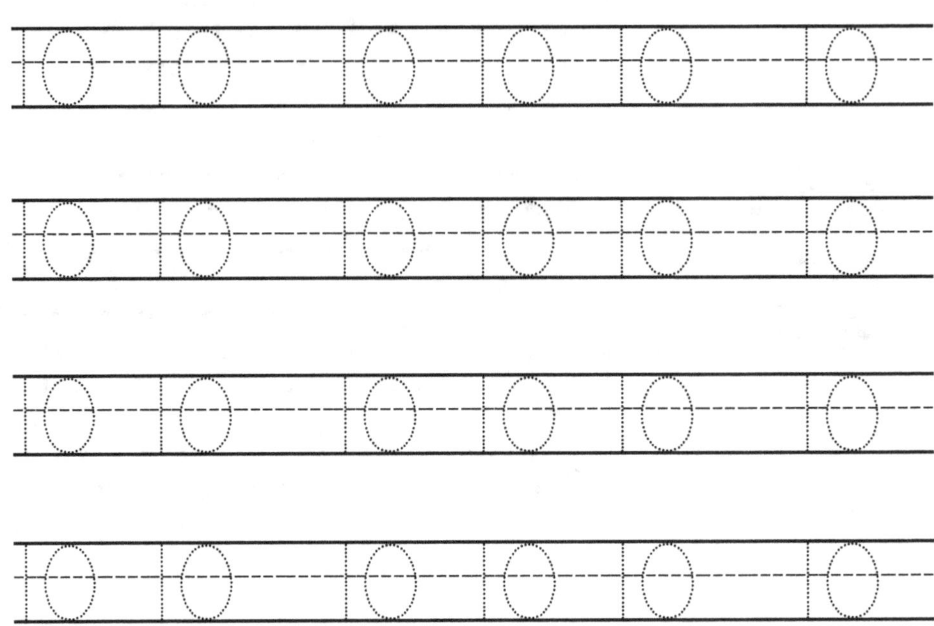

Trace the word Ten

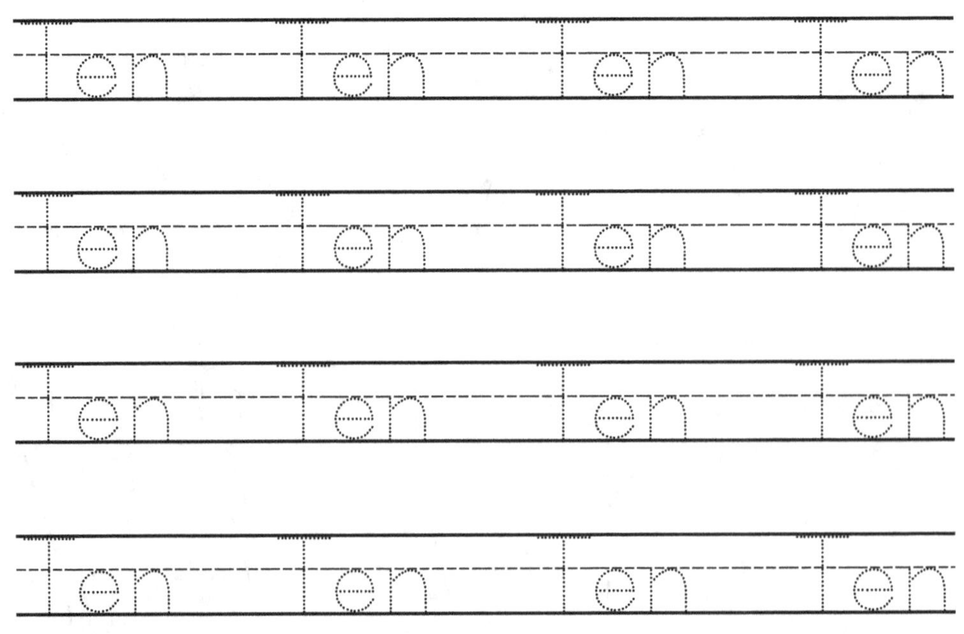

10

Write Number 10

10
10
10
10

Ten

Color Ten Cherries

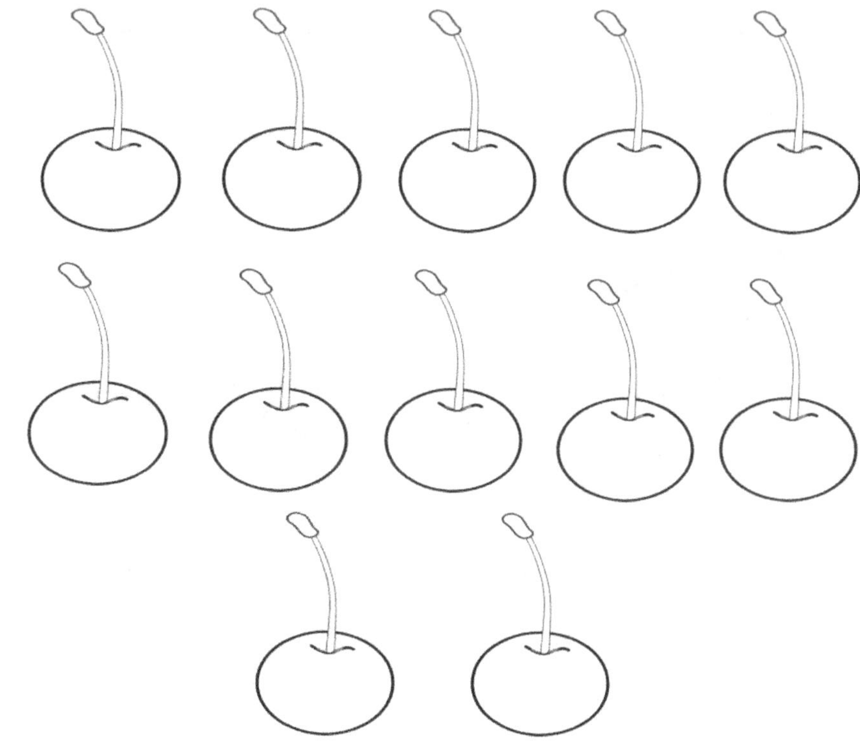

There are 8 oranges on the plate. Five are yellow and the rest are green.

a) Colour in the oranges.
b) Fill in the missing numbers.

| 5 | + | | = | |

| 8 | - | | = | |

What has happened to the tub of 10 strawberries?
Complete the equations.

$9 - 2 + 3 =$ ☐ $9 - 3 - 4 =$ ☐

Write the correct numbers and color it.

Continue the colouring pattern.

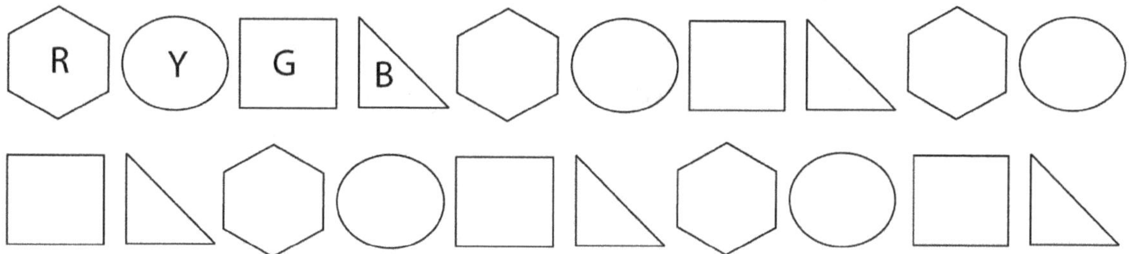

R = Red
Y = Yellow
G = Green
B = Blue

Colour the first shape **blue**, the second and the third shapes **green**,
then the fourth **blue** and the next two shapes **green**, and so on.

a. $1 + 2 + 1 + 2 + 1 + 2 + 1 =$

b. The number of red shapes is:

The number of blue shapes is:

The number of blue squares is:

The number of red squares is:

Complete the words!

cake   bike   corn   honk

c			e
	o	n	
b			
		r	

Complete the words!

sock   stop   worm   join

Complete the words!

blue   frog   shop   kiss

b   e

h   p

k

o

Complete the words!

wing   ship   feet   king

f   t

      h   p

w

                n

Complete the words!

soap   play   gift   rain

soap	play	gift	rain
p			y
	i		
r			
		a	

MATCH THE VEGETABLES

Write the name of the correct vegetable and then color them in!

BROCCOLI ONION TURNIP MUSHROOM CORN PEPPER

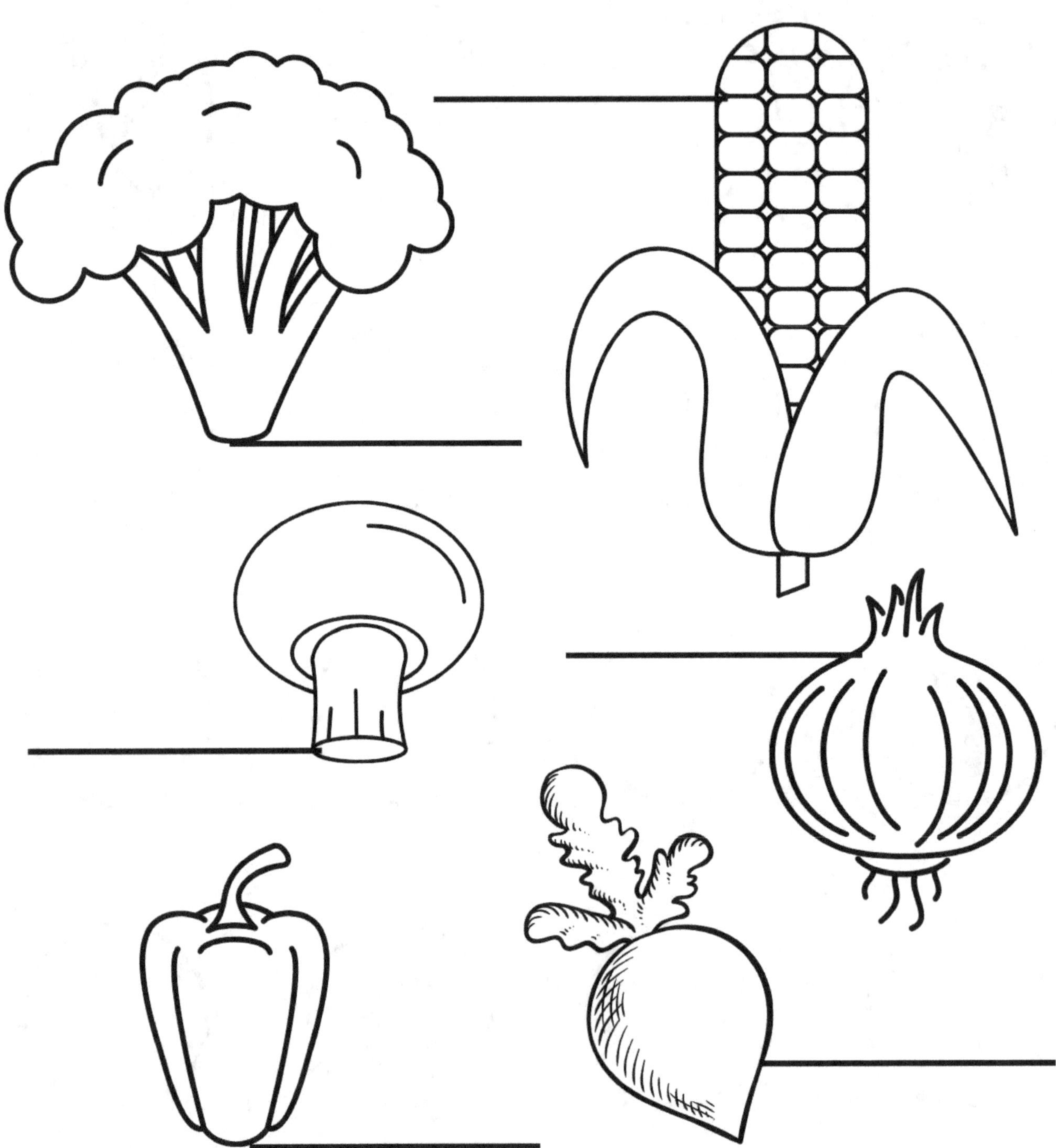

MATCH THE FRUITS

Write the name of the correct fruit and then color them in!

STRAWBERRY GRAPES BANANA PINEAPPLE WATERMELON CHERRY

MATCH THE PLANTS

Write the name of the correct plant and then color them in!
CACTUS ROSE SUNFLOWER DANDELION DAISY TULIP

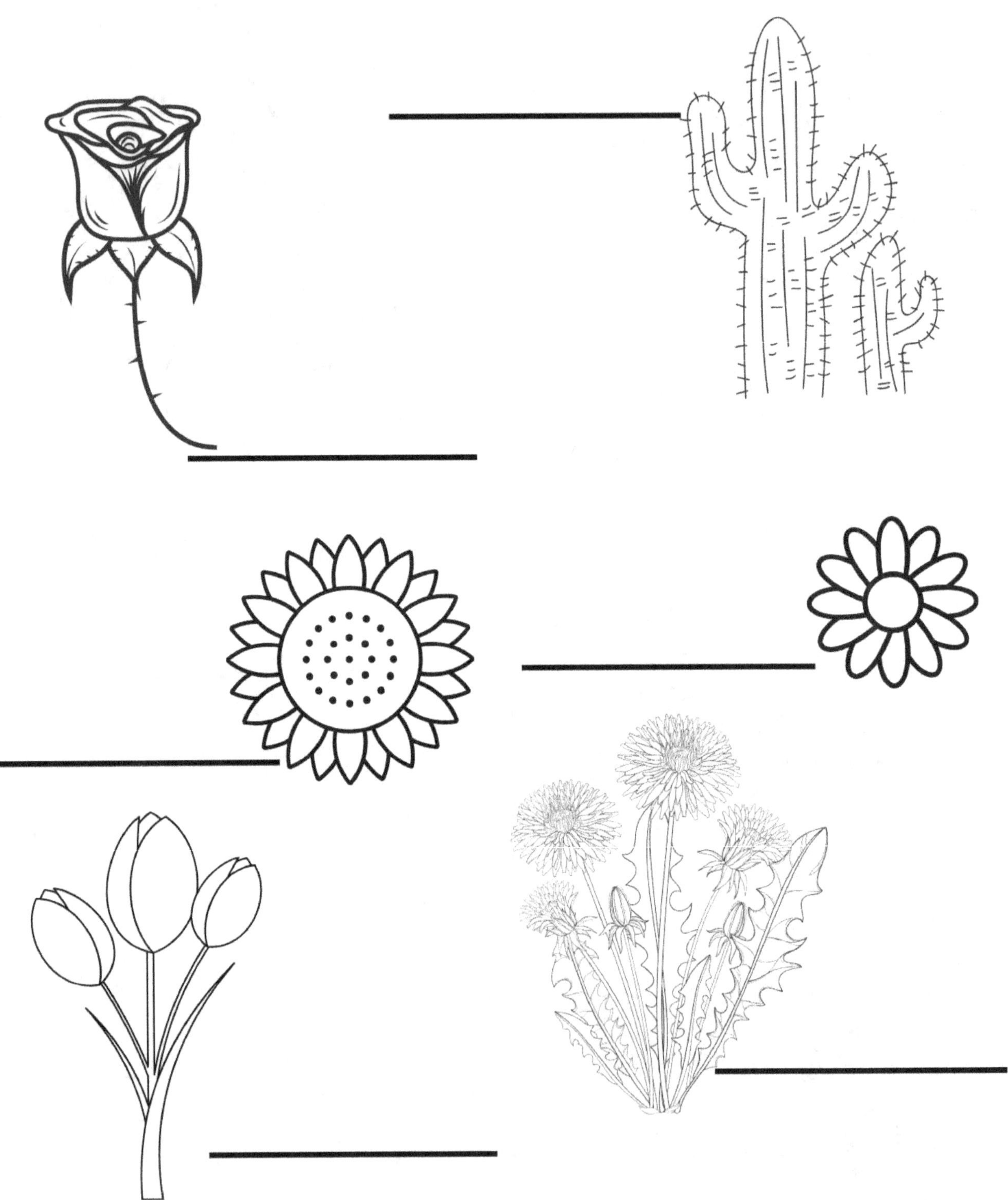

MATCH THE FOODS

Write the name of the correct food and then color them in!

PASTA BREAD HAMBURGER ICE CREAM CUPCAKE CHICKEN

MATCH THE ANIMALS

Write the name of the correct animal and then color them in!

CAT MONKEY SHARK RABBIT SPIDER CROCODILE

A______________________________________

a______________________________________

B________________________

b________________________

C
C

D_____________________

d_____________________

E_____________________

e_____________________

F______________________

f______________________

G__________________________

g __________________________

H____________________________

h____________________________

I________________________

i________________________

J ___________________________

j ___________________________

K＿＿＿＿＿＿＿＿＿＿＿＿＿＿＿＿＿

k＿＿＿＿＿＿＿＿＿＿＿＿＿＿＿＿＿

M______________

m______________

N______________________

n______________________

O____________________

o____________________

P___________________

p___________________

Q________________________________

q________________________________

R______________________

r______________________

S__________________________

s__________________________

T____________________

t____________________

U_________________________

u_________________________

V______________________________

v______________________________

W______________________
w______________________

X_______________________________

X_______________________________

Y________________________

y________________________

Z_________________________

Z_________________________